Forging Strength Overcoming Challenge

Author: Hussein Abdi

Copyright © 2025 Hussein Abdi

Table of Contents

Forging Strength

Overcoming Challenges

Preface

This book is for the people who weren't supposed to make it.

For the ones who came from nothing.

For the ones who were counted out.

For the ones who've had to fight—quietly, daily, without applause.

Some of these pages are my story.

Some are principles I live by.

Some are things I wish someone had told me earlier.

I didn't write this for likes.

I didn't write this to sound smart.

I wrote this because I had to.

Where I come from, people don't expect you to be sitting in a café writing a book—especially not someone like me.

But I'm here.

Still standing.

Still locked in.

I look up to people like David Goggins because he didn't just talk about discipline—he lived it.

And even though he does not know me, his mindset helped shape mine.

This book is not fake inspiration.

It is real.

It is direct.

It is what got me through war zones, tough streets, and silent battles.

And now?

It's yours.

Use it.

Challenge yourself.

Pass it down.

Because someone in your life needs to know that giving up is not an option.

And neither is going back.

Let us begin.

Chapter 1: Desperate Choices

Growing up in Somalia meant living two separate lives.

Inside our home, there was warmth. My mother filled the rooms with love. She taught high school chemistry and made even tough lessons feel easy. My father was quiet but strong. His hands were always dirty with grease, but he kept the cars moving and the family steady.

Outside the house, nothing felt steady. The country was falling apart.

One evening, something shifted. The air felt heavy. My mother's face changed before anything happened. She knew. Like a lion sensing danger before it strikes.

Then came the knock.

Loud. Angry. A knock that meant trouble.

My father stood up. Silent. Waiting. Outside the door, we heard voices—low, sharp, dangerous. Men with guns. Men who killed men like my father.

My mother didn't waste time. She handed him a small bundle of money. Her voice was low.

"Go."

He looked at her. No words. Just a nod. He kissed her cheek and slipped out the back window.

The front door slammed open.

Four men charged in. Rifles up. No questions. They wanted power, money, control. They tore through the house, flipping chairs, pulling out drawers, yelling.

One man—tall, stiff face—aimed his rifle at us. My brothers and I stayed still. I could hear Ali breathing fast beside me.

My mother stepped forward.

Her voice shook, but it didn't break. "We have nothing."

The man stared at her. His rifle didn't move.

She said it again. "We don't have anything."

He studied her tears, then lowered the rifle. "They don't have anything," he muttered. "Let's go."

But one of them looked at Ali. My brother had always been quiet. Strong. The kind of strength that gets mistaken for defiance.

"We're taking him."

11

My mother screamed. She grabbed Ali and held on with everything she had.

"Please! Don't take my son!"

No one moved. No one breathed. I thought they might kill us all.

But the leader raised his hand. "Leave them."

They walked out. Quick. Cold.

We didn't move until the last footstep faded.

My father climbed back through the window. He hugged us tight. He looked shaken, like someone who had seen a future he didn't like.

"We have to leave," he said. "This place isn't safe."

By sunrise, we were gone. No plan. Just survival

Chapter 2: The Treacherous Road to Freedom

The way to Kenya wasn't a road. It was survival.

We moved at night. No lights. No talking. Only the stars lit our path.

Fear followed us. It sat on our backs like weight we couldn't drop.

My father led. Always a few steps ahead. His eyes scanned everything—every shadow, every sound. He was ready to protect, ready to act.

The days punished us. The sun cooked our skin. The ground burned our feet. At night, the cold punished us differently. It slipped into our bones. Hunger chewed at our stomachs, and our legs begged to stop.

But we didn't stop.

Stopping wasn't safe.

Every sound in the forest had meaning. A branch snapped— was it an animal or a man with a gun? Wind moved the bushes—was it wind or something else?

We walked anyway.

We stayed close. Every few minutes, my mother whispered prayers. Her voice stayed calm, even when nothing else felt calm. Those prayers helped.

One night, my legs gave out. Just buckled. I couldn't go anymore.

"I can't," I said, barely loud enough to hear myself.

My father didn't speak. He didn't scold. He picked me up. Lifted me onto his shoulders like I weighed nothing.

"We're almost there," he said. "You're strong, like your mother."

He carried me through the night.

I didn't just feel the muscles in his back. I felt the weight he carried. All of it. The stress. The fear. The responsibility. He didn't complain once.

That night, I learned that strength isn't about seeking attention. It's not about looking tough. Real strength is silent. Real strength just keeps going.

After days of walking, we reached the Kenyan border.

Guards stood their, watching us. Suspicious. Exhausted. You could tell they'd seen hundreds of people like us. Maybe thousands.

My father didn't plead. He didn't try to explain our whole story.

He spoke calm. Clear. Firm.

They let us in.

We stepped into Kenya with nothing. But we were still together. Still breathing.

We lived in Kenya for a couple of years. Things started to feel normal again. Not perfect. But stable.

That's when my dad found a better opportunity in Dar es Salaam.

We moved again. This time, we weren't running. We were chasing something better.

Tanzania felt different. New language. New routines. Different food. The air smelled different. The streets moved at a different pace.

I couldn't speak English. Not one word. I couldn't even read the alphabet.

That's when my mom stepped in.

Every night after dinner, she sat with me on the floor. She used old papers and a pen.

"A... B... C..." she said slowly. "Now you."

I repeated it. I wrote it down. My handwriting was sloppy, but I was trying.

She was patient. Every letter. Every sound.

"B is for boy."

"D is for dog."

Some nights I got frustrated. I didn't get it. The letters didn't make sense. But she didn't stop, and neither did I.

That's how I started learning English. One letter at a time. One sound at a time. On the floor, next to my mother.

She taught me how to speak by teaching me the alphabet.

Life got better.

I made some friends. Started going to class again. I was quiet, but I paid attention. I didn't want to mess up the second chance we had.

Then one afternoon, things changed.

I went to the supermarket alone. I don't remember why. I just remember taking a wrong turn.

That's when I saw the pickup truck.

Four men inside.

They looked at me. Locked eyes. I didn't even wait.

They hit the gas. Came straight at me.

I ran.

I didn't think. I didn't plan. My body just moved.

My heart pounded so fast I thought it would explode.

I never knew I could run that fast. Not in Somalia. Not in Kenya. Not anywhere.

I sprinted through streets I didn't know. I didn't stop until I hit a busy area. People. Stalls. Locals shouting prices.

That's when the pickup turned around and drove off.

I was soaked in sweat.

A man pulled me aside. He had seen the whole thing.

"You have to be careful," he said. "Those guys? Cannibals. They'll eat you alive."

I don't know if he was serious. I didn't ask.

But I never forgot it.

After that, I locked in.

School. Homework. Routine. I became a better student. More focused.

The walk to school had its own issues.

There was a massive tree along the path. Big trunk. Thick branches. Looked like something from a movie.

What I didn't know at first—it was crawling with spiders.

Not small ones. Big ones. Spiders the size of your hand.

The first time I passed under that tree, I didn't see them. Then I felt something drop on my neck. Then another on my shoulder.

I looked up.

They were falling.

All I could do was move—fast.

I swatted them off and kept running. My skin crawled the whole time. I couldn't stop scratching. Couldn't stop checking my clothes.

That tree became a symbol for me. Sometimes danger just waits, quiets, until you walk by.

We liked Tanzania. But the area we lived in had problems.

People were deep into black magic. It wasn't hidden. It was part of the culture in that area.

My parents weren't comfortable with it.

One night, my dad said, "We're leaving."

He didn't want to risk our safety. Not again.

He booked us on a massive ship. It was huge—looked like the Titanic to me.

We left Dar es Salaam and sailed to Mombasa.

The ship ride felt long. But it was calm. I remember standing near the railing and watching the ocean.

I remember thinking, maybe things are finally getting better.

From Mombasa, we took a bus to Uganda.

That's where we stayed.

Until we came to the U.S.

Chapter 3: A Fragile Refuge

Uganda gave us a chance to breathe.

We didn't live in a refugee camp. We had a house. It wasn't big. It wasn't perfect. But it had walls, a roof, and a front door that locked.

That alone made it feel like a gift.

My father worked hard to make that possible. He picked up any job he could find. Mostly fixing cars. Sometimes working construction. If it paid, he did it.

We didn't have much, but we had what we needed. Food.
Clothes. A place to sleep.

That was more than we'd had before.

My older brothers went to school.

They were serious. Focused. They woke up early, packed their
notebooks, and came home talking about what they'd learned.

But I was different.

I couldn't sit still. I couldn't focus.

The school building felt like a box I didn't fit in.

Outside felt better.

I started skipping school. I wandered the neighborhood. I
found kids who did the same. We played soccer in the street.
Climbed trees. Got into trouble.

The world felt wide, and I didn't want to be trapped in a
classroom.

My mother found out quickly.

She didn't hit me. She didn't raise her voice.

She walked straight to the school the next morning.

She told the teachers, "Discipline him. Do what you need to."

And they did.

They embarrassed me. Made me stand in front of the class. Gave me extra chores.

So I left.

I ran back to the street. Back to freedom.

The next day, I got a letter.

I was expelled.

My mom didn't scream.

She stood in the kitchen. Arms crossed. Eyes locked on mine.

"If you won't learn from them," she said, "you'll learn from me."

And that was it.

She became my teacher.

Every morning, she woke me up early. She didn't ask if I was ready.

She opened her notebook. She handed me a pencil.

First, she taught me the alphabet.

We started with A, B, C.

She pointed at each letter and made me repeat it.

She wrote words. I copied them.

Some letters confused me. Some sounds didn't make sense.

But she didn't stop. She didn't let me stop either.

She made me repeat the same things until I could say them without thinking.

After letters came words.

After words came sentences.

She didn't teach with emotion. She taught with discipline.

If I got lazy, she snapped her fingers and told me to sit up.

If I got frustrated, she said the same thing every time:

"You will be something one day."

Her voice was calm. But her eyes were serious.

That sentence stuck with me more than anything else I learned.

I started improving.

I could sound out words.

I could write my name clearly.

I started asking questions. Not just about English, but about how things worked. Why things were the way they were.

My mother answered every question with focus.

Sometimes she'd pause. Think. Then explain it in a way I could understand.

She didn't just want me to memorize things.

She wanted me to understand them.

One afternoon, after a long study session, I laid on the floor of our living room.

I stared out the window.

A plane crossed the sky above us.

I watched it until it disappeared behind the clouds.

That was the first time I said it out loud:

"One day, I'll be on a plane too."

Not just to leave.

But to go somewhere I belonged.

To prove I could go further than anyone thought I could.

To make my mother proud.

To make her work mean something.

Chapter 4: The Land of Opportunity

The day we learned we were moving to the United States didn't feel real.

It came quietly.

No big announcement. No celebration.

Just a piece of news that sat in the room like a question.

My father walked in holding a letter. He said we'd been approved.

We looked at him like he was joking.

"Approved for what?" my brother asked.

"To go to America," my father said.

No one moved.

My mother sat down, her hand covering her mouth. "Is this really happening?" she asked. Her voice was soft. Her eyes didn't blink.

None of us said a word.

We had known families who waited years. Some never got accepted. Some applied again and again.

Now it was happening to us.

A woman named Emily—someone we had never met—had sponsored our family.

She was part of a church organization that helped families like ours.

She didn't owe us anything. She didn't even know our names before that moment.

But she chose us.

She saw our story, and for reasons we may never fully understand, she helped.

That kind of kindness stays with you.

It changes how you see the world.

For what she did for our family, I am deeply grateful.

She became part of our family.

Leaving Uganda wasn't easy.

We packed everything we had into three small bags.

My mother cleaned every room in our house before we left. She said, "Always leave a place better than you found it."

I think it was her way of showing respect.

She wanted to honor what that house gave us, even if we were moving on.

We said goodbye to neighbors, to friends, to what had become familiar.

The night before we left, I didn't sleep.

I laid on the floor and stared at the ceiling.

I thought about planes. I thought about what school might be like. I wondered if people in America would treat me different.

The airport was chaos.

Security checks. Papers. Questions. Lines.

When I saw the plane for the first time, my stomach flipped.

It was huge. Bigger than I expected.

Inside, everything felt cold and clean.

We buckled up. I looked out the window.

The engine started. I gripped the armrest.

When the plane lifted off, I felt like we were being pulled out of one life and dropped into another.

The land shrank. The clouds opened up.

I didn't blink for a long time.

We had a layover in Germany.

Everything moved fast. The language was different. People didn't smile much.

That's where it happened.

My younger brother wandered off.

One second he was right beside us. The next, he was gone.

We spread out in every direction. My father shouted his name. My mother looked like she couldn't breathe.

I checked every hallway. Looked under seats. Nothing.

My father found him curled up on a chair near a vending machine, fast asleep.

He picked him up without saying a word.

We were too tired to even talk about it.

When we landed in the U.S., it was early.

The airport was calm. The lights were soft. The air felt dry and clean.

Instead of Emily, one of her assistants was there to meet us.

She introduced herself kindly, helped with our bags, and drove us to the house Emily had arranged for us.

She told us Emily would visit the next day after we had time to rest.

The house was simple but felt like something new.

White walls. Empty rooms. A quiet street.

We each picked a room and sat together on the floor. My father led a prayer.

It didn't feel like home yet, but it felt safe.

The next morning, Emily came to see us.

She pulled up and stepped out of her car with that same kind smile.

She brought clothes. School supplies. Basic things we hadn't asked for—but needed.

She walked into the house like someone coming home.

We ran to the door to greet her.

We gave her a huge hug—all of us at once.

I tried to tell her thank you.

But my English was so broken, I stumbled through the words.

She just smiled and hugged me tighter.

She understood what I meant, even if I couldn't say it right.

She didn't know us. But she came prepared.

It wasn't just what she brought.

It was how she showed up.

With presence. With care. With time.

She didn't talk much about herself.

She focused on us.

That's what made it real.

.

That morning changed how I saw the world.

It made me believe that not everyone looks away when you need help.

Some people lean in.

Emily leaned in.

She didn't give us a new life.

But she gave us the chance to build one.

And that meant everything.

Chapter 5: New Beginnings in a Foreign Land

Starting school in America felt like stepping onto another planet.

Everything looked different. Everything sounded different. Everything felt unfamiliar.

I was twelve years old, placed in an elementary school where most of my classmates were younger. They played with toys and traded lunch snacks. I was trying to figure out how to say my name clearly.

Nobody explained how things worked. The rules were invisible. You were just supposed to know.

The biggest wall was the language.

English sounded overwhelming at first. Fast. Twisted. Hard to follow.

Teachers talked in full sentences. Students made jokes I didn't understand. Every word felt like a new kind of pressure.

I sat in class and watched their mouths move, trying to match sounds with gestures.

If someone pointed to the door and said "hall pass," I wrote it down. If someone yelled "fire drill," I watched how they lined up.

I was always watching. Always guessing.

The words didn't just confuse me—they made me feel small.

The first week, I said almost nothing.

I used hand signals. I nodded a lot. I smiled even when I didn't know what was going on.

Lunch was the easiest part of the day. Not because of the food, but because nobody expected you to talk.

I sat by myself at first.

Kids stared sometimes. A few came over to ask questions I didn't understand.

I just smiled again.

Winter came fast.

I had never seen snow before.

The world turned white. Soft. Quiet. Like something out of a movie.

I remember walking to the bus stop and touching snow for the first time. It didn't feel how I imagined. It was softer. Colder. Lighter.

That day I realized I didn't have the right coat. My fingers froze. My ears hurt. My lips cracked and bled.

That's when I learned about ChapStick.

I watched a classmate pull something from her backpack and rub it on her lips.

She smiled and passed it to another student.

So, I figured I would try it too.

The next day, I saw a tube in the classroom supply box. It looked just like what they were using.

I grabbed it, twisted the top, and smeared it all over my lips.

It felt thick. Sticky.

Too sticky.

One of the kids looked at me and said, "Bro… that's glue."

Everyone started laughing.

But not in a mean way. It wasn't cruel.

It was the kind of laugh you shared when something dumb happens to anyone.

Even I laughed, wiping the glue from my face.

That moment taught me something I never forgot—mistakes are part of learning.

Day by day, the language got easier.

I started picking up full sentences.

I could answer questions in class—even if my words were broken.

One afternoon, my teacher stopped everything. She told the class to listen.

"Go ahead," she said. "Say what you just said again."

I hesitated. Then I repeated it.

It wasn't perfect. My accent was heavy. I left out a word or two.

But she smiled like I had just said something brilliant.

Then the class clapped.

I wasn't expecting it. I didn't even know what to do.

So I bowed.

They laughed again—but this time it felt different.

For the first time, I felt like I belonged in that room.

We didn't stay in Memphis, Tennessee much longer after that.

After a few months or maybe a year, we moved to Columbus, Ohio.

It was colder. Bigger. But there was one big difference—there were more Somali families.

We found a small but growing community.

People spoke our language. They knew our culture. They understood things we didn't have to explain.

My parents felt more relaxed. You could see it in how they walked, how they talked to the neighbors.

We started attending a local mosque. My mother made friends. My father started helping people fix their cars again.

I focused harder on school.

I still struggled. But I wanted to prove I belonged. I wanted to make my mother proud.

She still woke me up early every day.

She still asked about my homework. Still made me read in front of her.

"You don't stop just because it's hard," she told me.

That sentence stayed with me. It still does.

In Columbus, I began to change.

I didn't just copy words—I understood them.

I didn't just go to school—I participated.

I still got nervous when I had to speak in front of the class.

But I did it anyway.

I still made mistakes.

But I stopped feeling embarrassed about them.

I knew what it felt like to be invisible.

I knew what it felt like to not be able to speak.

Now I had a voice.

I wasn't fluent yet. But I was learning fast.

And I was using it.

Chapter 6: The Call to Serve

After I graduated high school, I got a soccer scholarship to the University of Northwestern Ohio.

That felt like a big win. I was proud. My parents were proud. It was a full-circle moment—coming from where we started, to now being in college in a whole new world.

I didn't waste the opportunity.

I enrolled in the Diesel Technology program. I wanted something hands-on. Something real.

Engines made sense to me. You could take them apart, fix them, and see the results.

I earned my associate degree in Diesel. I had a trade. I had a skill. I had something I could use for life.

After school, things were good.

I had a solid job working on trucks. I bought a car. I had my own place.

No roommates. No drama. Just peace.

For a while, I thought this was it.

A stable life. A growing paycheck. A quiet routine.

But something in me started to itch. A voice in the back of my head kept asking: Is this it?

I tried ignoring it.

I tried telling myself I should be happy.

But I wasn't.

I knew things were good. I had stability. I had peace. But that wasn't enough for me. I decided to go back to school to learn more about mechanics. Then I enrolled again—this time for aircraft maintenance.

I've always loved fixing things. That's what I do. I like taking something that doesn't work, getting my hands on it, and making it better. There's something real about that.

I remember sitting in weight and balance class. Every component on the aircraft had to be measured. Every number mattered. The calculations weren't suggestions—they were requirements. Because if you got it wrong, even by a little, the whole plane could go down. That hit me. That kind of precision—that kind of responsibility—demanded your full focus.

Everything had to be torqued exactly to spec. Nothing was done from memory or guesswork. Every bolt, every adjustment, had to be verified against the maintenance manual. If it wasn't documented, it didn't happen. That's how strict the system was—and for good reason. Lives depended on it.

But even with that, I still wasn't satisfied. I wanted more. I was hungry—not for comfort, but for challenge. I didn't want to just fix things anymore. I wanted to test myself. I wanted to do everything.

After a few more classes, I made up my mind: once I finished them, I'd join the military.
I just didn't know what branch yet.

The truth is, I had always admired the people in uniform.

Military. Police. Firefighters. Anyone who served something bigger than themselves.

It wasn't about the power. It was about the discipline. The structure. The pride in showing up and doing the hard thing every day.

I remembered watching videos of Marines training. The obstacle courses. The shouting. The grit. I didn't see fear in their eyes—I saw focus.

That made an impact on me.

When I told some friends I was thinking about joining the military, they laughed.

"With your name? You think they'll take you?"

"Man, they'll ship you back before they ship you out!"

It stung. More than I let on.

I smiled it off. Laughed with them. Changed the subject.

But in my head, I'd already made up my mind.

They weren't going to understand. And that was fine.

Some things you have to do without explaining.

I moved in silence.

I didn't post about it. I didn't bring it up again.

I started researching.

I watched every video I could find on basic training. Army. Navy. Air Force. Marines.

I compared them.

I looked at the benefits. The lifestyle. The toughness. The stories.

Then one day, I drove to the recruiting station.

I walked in with a quiet mind and a serious heart.

The Army recruiters jumped at me first.

They were loud. Confident. Salesmen.

"Sign here and we'll get you a bonus."

"You'll be driving tanks, brother!"

I listened. I nodded.

But something felt off.

I didn't want to be sold.

I wanted to be tested.

As I turned to leave, I saw the Marine Corps office at the end of the hallway.

The door was half open. On the wall behind it was a poster that read:

"We don't accept applications—only commitments."

That line hit different.

It didn't feel like a job offer. It felt like a challenge.

I stepped in.

A Marine Staff Sergeant stood behind a desk.

He looked me in the eye and said, "What can I do for you?"

I told him, "I want something difficult."

He nodded once. Then reached into a drawer and pulled out three cards.

One said Education.

One said Travel.

One said Challenge.

"Pick the ones that matter to you," he said.

I picked all three.

He didn't smile.

He just said, "Then you're in the right place."

That day, I signed the papers.

I didn't tell anyone. Not my parents. Not my brothers. Not even my closest friends.

I wanted it to be mine.

My decision.

My risk.

My commitment.

Later that week, I sat my parents down.

We were in the living room. My mother was folding laundry. My father had just come in from work.

I looked at them and said, "I'm joining the Marines."

They both froze.

Then my father spoke. Calm. Serious.

"You're a grown man," he said. "This is your decision, and I respect it."

He didn't ask why. He didn't try to change my mind.

He just nodded like he already knew.

The night before I left, I finally told my friends.

They were shocked.

Some thought I was joking.

One of them said, "You? The Marines? No way."

"I ship out tomorrow," I said.

That shut them up.

That night, I laid on my bed and stared at the ceiling.

No TV. No music. Just silence.

I thought about the contract I had signed. The people I was leaving behind. The uniform I was about to wear.

I knew it wouldn't be easy.

But I didn't want easy.

I wanted to find out what I was really made of.

Chapter 7: The Yellow Footprints

The ride to the Marine Corps Recruit Depot was quiet at first.
Nobody talked. Nobody joked.
We all sat stiff in our seats, staring at the floor or the backs of
each other's heads. Most of us didn't know what was coming.
But we knew it wasn't going to be easy.

The moment we passed through those gates, the air changed.
You could feel it.
The tension inside the bus thickened like smoke. The silence?
It wasn't calm anymore. It was fear.

Then the bus driver barked: "Heads down!"
Everyone snapped to it. Eyes on the floor. Backs locked
straight. No one dared move.
Seconds later, the door slammed open like it had been kicked.
A drill instructor stormed in—loud, aggressive, locked in.
His voice hit like a grenade.
"GET OFF MY BUS!"

Chaos.
No order. No structure. Just boots hitting the pavement.
We spilled out fast, bumping into each other like scared
animals. No one wanted to be last.

And then I saw them.

The yellow footprints.

Painted right there on the pavement—waiting for us.

Dozens of them. Two feet per set. Spaced perfectly apart.

We were told to line up. One recruit per set.

No thinking. No questions. Just stand where you're told.

That was the moment everything shifted.

That's where it started.

That's where the transformation began.

You don't forget the yellow footprints. Ever.

They mark the line between who you were—and who you're about to become.

You stand there, and your name stops mattering.

So does your story. Your accent. Your past.

None of it counts anymore.

You're not a person anymore.

You're a recruit.

You're part of a group now.

You move together. Breathe together. Get punished together.

And if one person messes up, the whole unit pays.

Boot camp was everything I expected—and worse.

Physically, it was brutal.

We ran everywhere. Pushups. Pullups. Hikes with gear.
Obstacle courses. Sand pits. No breaks. No comfort.

Your body gets sore and stays sore.
But that's the easy part.
The real fight? That's mental.
The grind. The doubt. The constant pressure to quit. That's
what separates people.
That's what breaks the ones who came in soft.

Every morning, I repeated the same line in my head:
"Easy day. We got this."
Not because it was easy.
But because I could not afford to let weakness in.
Not even for a second.

After graduation, I went to the School of Infantry.

We learned the basics of combat—how to shoot, move, and
communicate.

Rifle drills. Field exercises. Close-quarters tactics. Patrol
formations.

It was real training. Serious stuff.

Every round fired had a purpose.

You had to stay sharp or fall behind.

I liked it. It made sense to me.

After SOI, I went to Fort Leonard Wood, Missouri, for my MOS school.

It was different right away.

That base belonged to the Army.

And they did things differently.

Rules were looser. Schedules were softer. Structure felt lighter.

We stayed there for three months learning how to drive tactical vehicles.

Convoy ops. Gear checks. Licensing. Emergency scenarios.

The learning was good. But the culture felt off.

Compared to the Marine Corps, it was slower. Less intense.

Still, we made the most of it.

On off-days, we'd hit the MCX and load up on junk food—
chips, soda, whatever we could afford.

Those small things kept us going.

Sometimes, all you needed was a cold drink and something
salty to feel like a person again.

After graduation, I got my orders for the fleet.

Checked in to my first real unit.

That's where things got interesting.

Not everyone was happy to see a new motivated Marine.

Some staff members had been around too long. They got
lazy. Comfortable.

I showed up trying to do everything. Volunteering. Helping.
Asking questions. Staying in shape.

They didn't like that.

One staff member pulled me aside and said:

"If you joined the Marine Corps just to go to college, you
joined the wrong branch."

I didn't argue.

But in my head, I knew he was wrong.

I was driven.

That's who I was.

I wasn't just trying to serve—I was trying to grow.

That's why I signed up to become a range coach.

It gave me purpose. It kept me sharp. It let me help other Marines get better with their weapons.

It also showed the leadership that I was serious.

I wanted more than a paycheck.

I wanted to earn everything I touched.

One of the coolest things I ever did in the Marine Corps was underwater training.

They flip a tactical vehicle with you inside—windows shut, water pouring in.

You're strapped in. Upside down. No light.

And you have to find a way out.

That training sent my adrenaline through the roof.

I could feel my heartbeat in my ears. My lungs squeezed tight.

That water gets cold, fast.

You don't panic. You solve the problem.

It reminded me of back home—being chased as a kid and still survived.

Same pressure. Same focus.

You don't freeze.

You move.

Within the Marine Corps, I had a lot of mentors.
But one of them stood out the most.
1st Sergeant Juan L. Garcia.

He didn't yell to be heard.
He didn't use rank to get respect.
He led by example.

He carried himself like a man who earned everything the hard way.

His words stuck with me. Especially this:

"Remember these three things:
Do not allow your Senior Enlisted Advisor to make a recommendation to take away your pay or rank.
Do not give a Commissioned Officer the opportunity to take away your pay or your rank.
Protect what you've earned. You earned it—you put in the work."

That hit different.
He wasn't just talking about rank.
He was talking about everything—your time, your effort, your reputation.
"Protect what you've earned."
That became my mindset.
Not just in the Marine Corps—but in life.

1st Sergeant Juan L. Garcia truly cared about his Marines. He was the kind of leader who would reach out and say,

"Brother, if there are any Marines at the barracks, please send them to my house. I don't want Marines to be there for the holidays."

Every holiday, he made sure Marines weren't left alone in the barracks. If there were no formal events, he asked the sergeants to send them to his house. We'd grill. We'd bond. The whole platoon became tight—like a family.

The barracks can get real depressing, especially on holidays when you can't be with loved ones. But because of him, we didn't feel that isolation.

1st Sergeant Juan L. Garcia was the blueprint for what real leadership looks like.

He used to say during safety briefs:

"Allow me to be your sword. Let me be your shield from everything that's happening above us."

He wasn't just protecting us—he was building us.

During every field op, he would pull me aside and ask,

"What kind of leader will you be when you become a noncommissioned officer?"

At first, I thought being an NCO meant being a fierce bulldog. But every time, he'd correct me.

"That's not the kind of leader your Marines need. Be someone they'll look up to."

I did look up to him. I told myself—if I ever got promoted, I'd carry myself like he did.

And the day I got pinned?

It was an honor to get pinned by him.

I remember one of The company First Sergeant pulled me aside and asked who was pinning me. When I said his name, he smiled.

You could tell he knew him back in the day—and respected him too.

If it weren't for 1st Sergeant Juan L. Garcia, I wouldn't have carried myself the way I did.

He gave me a blueprint. He gave me the standard.

And I held on to it.

If you're ever reading this, 1st Sergeant Juan L. Garcia—I want you to know how much I truly respected you. I'm beyond grateful for everything you did, not just for me, but for the entire platoon. The way you led, the way you showed up for us, the way you protected and challenged us—it left a mark that will never be forgotten. You didn't just lead Marines. You inspired us. You changed the way we carried ourselves. And for that, I thank you. You were one of the finest leaders I've ever known, and it was an honor to serve under you. I hope this brings a smile to your face, because every word came from the deepest respect.

Chapter 8: What the Marines Taught Me

The Marine Corps didn't just change me. It revealed who I already was.

It took the drive I had—and sharpened it.

It took my discipline—and doubled it.

It took my flaws—and forced me to face them.

You don't get to hide in the Marine Corps.

Not behind excuses. Not behind other people.

You show up. You perform. Or you don't.

One of the biggest things I learned was pressure doesn't break you. It builds you.

Back home, I knew pressure—being chased, being tested, being pushed to survive.

But the Marines taught me how to operate under it.

How to stay calm when everything's loud.

How to lead when no one else will.

How to take orders without losing your identity.

How to earn respect—not demand it.

I learned that discipline beats motivation.

Motivation comes and goes.

Some mornings, I didn't feel like doing anything.

I didn't feel like running. I didn't feel like standing in formation. I didn't feel like being screamed at by someone who barely knew my name.

But I showed up.

Every time.

That's discipline.

You do the work even when you don't want to.

I learned how to lead by example.

You don't need to be the loudest.

You don't need to be the one giving orders.

Sometimes, being the one who shows up early, carries extra gear, helps the guy next to you—that's enough.

I didn't always speak first, but people noticed how I moved.

That mattered more.

I learned how to fail.

Sometimes you mess up.

You forget gear. You fall behind on a run. You miss a detail.

You take the hit. You fix it. You move on.

No complaining. No blame.

You grow fast when you learn to own your mistakes.

Most of all, I learned that nothing is promised—not the job, not the rank. Not the outcome.

You can train hard. Do everything right.

Then one bad call, one missed step, and everything changes.

That's why you stay ready.

That's why you do it for the right reasons.

You don't serve for praise.

You serve because you believe in the standard.

Because it makes you better.

Everything I learned in the Marine Corps shaped how I live now.

How I train. How I plan. How I treat people.

How I carry myself when nobody's watching.

I keep my word.

I don't cut corners.

I don't give up under pressure.

And I never forget where I came from.

Chapter 9: The Transition

Leaving the Marine Corps was harder than I expected.
Not the paperwork. Not the logistics.
The mindset.

When you wear that uniform every day, it becomes part of you. Your schedule, your attitude, your decisions—all shaped by it.
Then one day, you wake up and it's over.
No formation. No uniform. No mission.
Just silence.

The day I got out, I looked in the mirror and didn't feel different.
But everything around me had changed.
No chain of command. No orders.
I was back on my own again.
I had to make my own structure. My own rules. My own accountability.

A lot of guys struggle with that.

They lose the routine. Then they lose their grip.

For me, I leaned back on what got me through everything else:

Discipline.

If no one else was going to hold me to a standard, I would.

I still woke up early.

I still trained.

I still planned every day the night before.

The biggest thing I noticed after getting out?

People complain too much.

They waste time.

They make excuses.

They act like life is supposed to be easy.

But I already knew—it's not.

Life doesn't care how tired you are.

It keeps going. You either keep up or get left behind.

Inside the Corps, things are clear.

You speak bluntly. You move fast. You don't sugarcoat anything.

You don't tiptoe around feelings. You get the job done and keep moving.

Out here? It's different. You have to think twice before you speak.

You can say something that was totally normal in the military—and now it gets taken the wrong way.

People don't understand the lingo. They don't get the tone.

They take things literally.

What used to be everyday speech in the Corps can land you in trouble on the outside.

I had to unlearn some of that.

Tone it down. Read the room.

Not because I was ashamed of being a Marine, but because I had to adapt.

That's part of the transition, too—learning when to leave certain habits behind.

Not the discipline. Not the toughness.

But the lingo? The short fuse? The sarcasm?

That stuff doesn't always translate.

Sometimes you have to bury that language with the uniform.

Some people expected me to slow down after I left the military.

They thought I'd sit back. Relax.

They were wrong.

Getting out was never the end for me.

It was just another beginning.

I started using the GI Bill.

This time, I wasn't studying engines or tactical vehicles.

I went back to school for something different—health care.

My goal is to become an MRI tech.

I want to help people. I want a skill that matters.

The body is like a machine, and I want to learn how to read it from the inside out.

I've seen injuries. I've seen pain. Now I want to understand what causes it and how to spot it.

One day in class, I had another Marine sitting with me. He'd just gotten out too—retired after 20 years.

The teacher was going through PowerPoint after PowerPoint. You know the type—death by slides.

Then the instructor said, "Be back in class in 15 minutes."

Without thinking, the Marine next to me barked out, "KILL!"

That's how we used to say roger that in the Corps. Just a habit.

But the instructor froze.

He said, "Sir, we need to notify law enforcement. We take every threat very seriously."

Me and the other Marine looked at each other.

He quickly said, "Sir, I apologize. I didn't mean it like that— it's just something we always said."

That moment stuck with me.

It showed how far removed we were from civilian life—and how careful we had to be.

The world we came from didn't always translate out here.

Most people don't expect someone like me—ex-Marine, diesel guy, range coach—to choose health care.

But I've never followed the path people expected.

I follow the one that makes sense to me.

Helping people. Using tech. Staying disciplined.

That's where I'm headed.

You don't leave the Marines the same way you came in.

And you don't walk away from that experience without carrying something with you.

For me, it wasn't just a title or a story.

It was a standard.

A way of showing up to life.

No shortcuts. No begging. No backdoors.

Just effort.

Every day.

Chapter 10: Self-Leadership

In the military, someone's always telling you what to do.

Be here at this time.

Wear this. Carry that. Move like this. Speak like that.

There's no confusion.

Everything is direct. Structured. Tightly controlled.

Then one day, it's just… gone.

No orders.

No structure.

Just you, your thoughts, and whatever choices you make.

That's where most people slip.

They lose the uniform and forget the discipline.

They forget how to lead themselves.

But I didn't forget.

I couldn't.

I knew that if I let up, even for a day, it would start to stack.

One skipped workout turns into a week.

One missed assignment turns into dropping the ball.

One excuse turns into two.

Next thing you know, you're not you anymore.

So I built my own system.

Woke up early.

Trained even when I didn't feel like it.

Made my own schedule.

Planned my weeks out in advance.

Tracked progress—physically, mentally, and academically.

Every Sunday night, I sat down and mapped the week ahead.

Nobody told me to.

But that's the difference between being pushed… and pushing yourself.

Self-leadership means doing the work when nobody's watching.

It means holding yourself accountable when nobody would even know you skipped.

It means staying mission-focused even when their's no threat.

I didn't need someone yelling in my ear anymore.

That voice was already in my head—and it had my back.

Every time I wake up tired and still train, I prove to myself I'm in control.

Every time I study instead of wasting time, I prove I still want it.

Every time I choose to show up instead of take the easy way out, I keep the old me alive—the one who never quit, never waited, and never blamed anyone.

Some days, it's harder than others.

You don't always feel strong.

You don't always feel motivated.

But you still move.

That's the difference between most people and the ones who really get it.

The ones who win long-term aren't driven by how they feel.

They're driven by who they are.

I don't have a rank anymore.

I don't have a title stitched onto my chest.

But I carry myself the same way I did in uniform.

Head high. Eyes sharp. Feet moving.

Because self-respect doesn't come from what you wear.

It comes from what you do.

Chapter 11: Pressure Is a gift

People think life gets easier once you've been through the worst of it. It doesn't. It just changes form. Out here, adversity doesn't yell in your face or chase you down a dirt road. It shows up quiet. Bills. Deadlines. Family stuff. A bad grade. A failed test. Disrespect at work. Health scares. Setbacks that don't make headlines. You don't see it coming. But it's there. And you either face it—or break.

For me, pressure is normal. I've lived under it my whole life. Running through the woods in Somalia. Moving country to country. Carrying my family's hope. Going through boot camp. Getting flipped in underwater training. Leading myself in silence. Pressure was always there. Now I see it differently. Pressure is a gift not a curse. It means you've been trusted with something that matters. It means the moment is bigger than your comfort. And if you feel it—it means you're still in the game.

I still hear David Goggins in my head. "Stay hard." "Callous your mind." "You don't know me, son!"

That energy shaped me. He taught me that pain is where growth lives. That weakness doesn't get a say unless you give it one. That nobody's coming to save you. That suffering is the test—and you either pass it or stay the same.

I carry that mindset every day. When I hit the books for my anatomy classes and I'm tired—I keep going. When I'm up at 5 a.m. and it's freezing—I lace my shoes and train.

When life throws problems at me back-to-back—I solve them one by one. I don't wait to feel ready. I don't pray for it to get easier. I just go.

Pain doesn't scare me anymore. Failure doesn't scare me. Comfort does. Comfort is what ruins people. They stop trying. Stop pushing. Stop growing. They get soft. Passive. Weak in the mind. That's the real threat.

Every challenge I face now—I ask myself one question: "What would the old me do?" Then I do better than that. Because that's the point. Every day is a chance to outdo the person you used to be. Not for attention. Not for applause. But because you said you would.

I'm literally writing a book right now because I want to defy the odds. Nobody expects me to be the guy sitting in the corner of some quiet coffee shop, full-time student, grinding through a memoir like this. But here I am. Doing it anyway. Not for the spotlight. But to prove something—to myself, to the younger version of me, to the next person like me. All you really need to know is this: Don't forget where you came from. And stay locked in.

When people can't stop you, they try to ignore you. They act like you're not doing something big. They downplay your effort. They pretend they don't see the grind. That's cool. Let them. Because once you become undeniable, they won't have a choice.

Being undeniable means your work speaks louder than opinions. It means your consistency outshines the doubt. It means no one can deny what you've done—because you've shown up too many times to be ignored. No excuses. No shortcuts. Nothing extra. Just results.

You don't need to announce every move. You don't need to prove anything to people who don't matter. You just need to be so locked in that your success shows up without asking permission.

You keep stacking wins while they keep talking. Let them doubt. Let them sleep. Let them gossip. And when it's time— let the results talk for you.

I wasn't supposed to be here. Not in the U.S. Not in the Marines. Not in college. This isn't about writing a book while just getting by in life. I'm doing this while going to school full-time, chasing a career in healthcare, keeping my circle small, and staying locked in on my vision. No shortcuts. No distractions. Just real effort, day in and day out.

But I'm here. And I didn't get here because someone handed it to me. I got here because I refused to give up.

People tried to tell me what I couldn't do. They still do. But I don't hear it anymore. Because I've been proving them wrong for too long to stop now. And I'm not looking for their approval—I'm building a life that doesn't need it.

And that's what it takes to be undeniable. It's not about being the strongest, smartest, or fastest. It's about being the most committed. The one who doesn't slip under pressure. The one who doesn't break when it gets quiet. The one who shows up—every single time.

I don't want to be liked. I want to be respected. And respect isn't given. It's earned. Earned through effort. Through pain. Through discipline. Through silence and sacrifice. Earned by being the person who didn't stop. That's what I'm building. Not hype. Not noise. Proof.

Be undeniable. Not by talking louder. But by working longer. And harder. And smarter. Until even the ones who doubted you have to admit— You did it. And they can't say a word.

Life doesn't hit you once and leave you alone. It keeps testing you. Sometimes back to back. Sometimes when you least expect it. And if you're not ready? You break. But if you've trained your mind to stay in the fight? You don't just survive. You bounce back harder.

That's what I've built. Not a perfect life. Not a flawless record. But a mindset that won't give up. A core that doesn't crack under pressure. A bounce-back so strong that setbacks don't scare me anymore—they just signal it's time to go harder.

I've lost before. I've failed. I've messed things up, made bad calls, missed opportunities. But I've never stayed down. Not once. Because I was never built to give up.

Every "L" I've taken? It taught me something. It gave me a mirror I couldn't ignore. It gave me a decision to make—stay soft or get sharper. And every single time, I chose to sharpen.

Resilience isn't just about staying alive. It's about locking in— even when motivation's gone. It's about feeling the pressure—and not letting it take your power. It's about rebuilding, even when you're tired of rebuilding. Because the alternative? Is giving up. And that's never been an option for me.

That's resilience. Doing the hard thing. Not because it feels good—but because you said you would. Because you know weakness is always looking for a way back in—and you don't give it an inch.

I don't fear failure. I fear staying the same. I fear living soft. I fear being comfortable when I should be growing. So I stay uncomfortable on purpose. I train for the bounce-back before I even fall.

You can take the hit. You can lose the job. You can get rejected. You can fall short. But if your mindset is right? You bounce back. Stronger. Smarter. Louder in silence. That's what I've trained for. That's what I live.

Because I know storms don't stop coming. So I stopped trying to avoid them. And I started becoming the kind of person who can walk through them without giving up.

Be resilient. Not just once. Every time. Because you don't need the perfect path. You just need the strength to keep coming back better. Every single time.

At the end of the day, you can dodge opinions. You can ignore advice. You can block the feedback. But there's one person you can't escape— yourself.

You know the truth. You know the effort you gave. You know if you skipped steps. You know if you gave 60% and called it 100.

You can wear motivation on your shirt. You can post it on your story. But you can't lie to yourself. You know what's real.

You want peace? Start earning it in private. Show up when nobody's checking. Do the hard things without applause. Keep your promises to yourself—daily. That's the kind of work your future self will thank you for.

Now every day, I check in. Check in—for accountability.

Did I show up? Did I move with purpose? Did I let myself off the hook?

Because I don't need anyone else's opinion. I just need to look myself in the eye and know I didn't let myself down. That's what self-respect looks like. That's what real progress feels like.

You can fake motivation. You can fake discipline online. You can fake effort in front of people. But consistency? That's different. You can't fake that. Not for long. Because consistency leaves proof.

You either: Show up. Or you don't. Keep your word. Or you don't. Build habits. Or keep breaking them.

The real ones? They don't need to say much. Their life speaks for them. Their results speak for them. Their presence speaks for them.

Because when you're truly consistent, you carry it. You walk differently. You move differently. You don't need to explain.

You built it through thousands of silent, disciplined reps. When nobody was clapping. When nobody believed. When no one saw.

That's how you know it's real. Not because it's posted. Not because it's praised. But because it never stops.

I don't care what you say you're gonna do. I care what you repeat. Once. Twice. Ten times. Fifty times. Every week. Every season.

That's how legacy is built. Not through talk. Not through one good day. But through reps.

You can fake a post. You can fake a quote. You can't fake consistency.

Chapter 12: Never Forget

I've lived in countries most people only hear about when it's bad news.

I've seen real struggle.

Not the kind where your Wi-Fi goes out or your coffee order is wrong.

I'm talking about real survival.

Guns at the door.

Running for your life.

Losing sleep because you're afraid of what might happen at night.

Watching your mother cry quietly and still cook dinner.

That kind of struggle never leaves you.

And I never want it to.

Because it keeps me grounded.

Every day I wake up and I remember where I came from.

That's not something I can ever afford to forget.

I'm not supposed to be here, statistically.

Not supposed to be in school.

Not supposed to be free.

Not supposed to have my own car, apartment, or be walking into a college classroom chasing a healthcare license.

People like me usually don't make it this far.

But I did.

And I don't take that lightly.

That's why I keep my circle small.

That's why I train like someone's watching me, even when they're not.

That's why I stay locked in.

Because I've seen what happens when you lose focus.

Life doesn't tap you on the shoulder.

It punches you in the mouth.

And if you're not ready, you'll get dropped.

I stay grateful, even when things get hard.

Grateful for the people who helped me, even the ones I don't talk to anymore.

Grateful for the teachers, the mentors, the recruiters, the staff who pushed me, corrected me, doubted me.

They all played a role.

Even the ones who didn't believe in me gave me fuel.

I think about my mother a lot when I'm working late on school assignments.

She never stopped believing in me.

Even when I messed up.

Even when I got expelled.

She kept pushing.

She knew something I didn't know yet—that I could do more.

Now I believe it too.

Some days I sit back and think about how far I've come.

From barefoot in the dirt to boots on parade deck to sneakers in a college hallway.

That's not luck.

That's not magic.

That's work.

Daily work.

Mental toughness. Physical effort. Personal responsibility.

Every version of me—young, scared, confused, disciplined, motivated—is still inside me somewhere.

And every day, I choose which one gets to show up.

So far, I've made the right choice.

This book is more than a story.

It's a statement.

It's proof that no matter where you come from or what your name is, you can rise.

Not by waiting.

Not by hoping.

But by deciding.

Chapter 13: Bigger Picture

Most people stop when things feel stable.

They get a decent job, a paycheck, a routine—and that's it.

They coast.

They slow down.

They shrink their world.

Not me.

I didn't survive everything I've been through just to play small now.

I see the bigger picture.

And I move like it.

Every day, I wake up with a reason.

Even on days when I'm tired.

Even when school gets overwhelming.

Even when I feel like nobody sees the effort.

I don't need validation.

I need progress.

I need momentum.

I need that next step.

Because I'm not trying to just live—I'm trying to build.

.

When I picture my future, I see results.

I see myself in a hospital or clinic, wearing scrubs, helping patients, running MRI scans, staying sharp.

I see someone walking in scared, confused, injured—and I'm the one that helps bring answers.

I want to be that.

That kind of calm. That kind of competence.

But I also know I won't get there by hoping.

It takes focus. Study. Patience. Reps.

Same way I trained in the Corps.

Same way I trained in life.

People think discipline stops once you leave the military.

That's false.

Discipline is portable.

It comes with you—if you keep feeding it.

Right now, my life is simple.

Class. Study. Train. Rest. Repeat.

It's not flashy. It's not fun all the time.

But it's real.

And I'm in it for the long game.

I've made it this far without shortcuts.

I'm not looking for one now.

I don't need a lucky break.

I need one more solid day stacked on top of the last one.

That's how I operate.

That's how I win.

Sometimes people ask me how I stay so focused.

"How do you stay motivated?"

I don't.

Motivation is nice, but it fades.

I stay locked in because I know what it feels like to have nothing.

And I know what it took to get here.

I'm not going backwards.

Not now. Not ever.

There's no finish line.

That's the truth.

You don't hit one goal and sit back.

You hit one goal—and use it as a launch pad for the next.

Life's too short to sit around just "getting by."

I'm not trying to survive anymore.

I'm trying to succeed.

Chapter 14: No Applause Needed

Most people want credit.

They want likes, shares, pats on the back, some kind of recognition for every move they make.

That's not me.

I don't need applause.

I don't need an audience.

I don't need people to understand why I do what I do.

Because I'm not doing it for them.

I train when no one's watching.

I study when no one's checking.

I grind in silence.

That's where the real wins come from.

The early mornings. The late nights. The moments where quitting sounds easier than finishing.

Nobody's around then.

That's when the decision really counts.

That's when you find out if your goals were real—or just talk.

People say they're tired.

I get tired too.

They say they don't have time.

I don't have time either—I make time.

They say, "I'll start Monday."

I say, "Start now."

Because nobody's coming to force you into greatness.

You either want it—or you don't.

When I go to class now, I sit near the front.

Not because I want to be seen.

Because I want to own the room quietly.

I take notes like I'm preparing for something bigger—
because I am.

I carry that same energy into workouts, into how I speak to
people, into how I carry myself at the gas station or the
grocery store.

Respect is a habit. So is focus.

So is discipline.

I'm not perfect.

But I hold myself accountable for everything.

If I mess up, I fix it.

If I'm wrong, I admit it.

If I'm behind, I catch up.

Because that's what a real man does.

He doesn't blame. He doesn't stall. He adjusts and moves
forward.

One thing I've learned: you don't owe anyone an explanation for your hunger.

They don't need to understand why you stay up late, why you run in the rain, why you write a book when nobody expects you to.

Let them doubt.

Let them guess.

You keep working.

When the results show up, they'll speak for themselves.

But even then—you don't stop.

You nod once.

Then you go back to work.

Because once you've tasted what progress feels like, you're never satisfied again.

No applause needed.

Just action.

Just forward.

Chapter 15: Stay Consistent

Motivation comes and goes.

Some days, it hits hard. You wake up ready. You train hard. You knock out every task like it's personal.

Then other days... nothing.

You don't feel like doing anything.

That's where most people fall off.

They let their feelings set the pace.

They only move when it feels good.

But that's not how I operate.

I don't chase highs. I chase consistency. ·

Because showing up when you feel like it? That's easy.

Showing up when you're tired, sore, pissed off, or behind schedule?

That's different.

That's discipline.

My life now isn't flashy.

It's built on the same blocks, repeated every day.

Wake up early.

Train. Eat. Study. Handle what needs to be handled.

Sleep. Repeat.

Simple doesn't mean easy.

But it works.

And I trust the process.

Consistency isn't about going 100 mph all the time.

It's about refusing to stop.

Even on your worst day, you give something.

Even when you fall short, you don't stay there.

You regroup. You come back.

That's what separates people.

Not talent. Not luck.

Discipline over time.

I remember being the kid who didn't know English.

Who had to learn the alphabet from his mom at the kitchen table.

I remember being the kid who ran from a pickup truck, heart pounding, thinking he was done for.

I remember standing on the yellow footprints, knowing this was make or break.

And now I'm here.

Still showing up.

Still chasing the next level.

Because the mission didn't stop.

It just changed uniforms.

You don't get consistent by accident.

You build it.

You earn it.

One hard choice at a time.

Wake up or hit snooze.

Cook or eat trash.

Study or scroll.

Lift or sit.

Lead or complain.

People say, "I don't have time."

They do.

They just don't manage it.

They waste it.

They let hours slip through their fingers, then act surprised when their life doesn't change.

Me?

I track time like it's money.

Because once it's gone, it doesn't come back.

You don't need to be perfect.

You just need to be reliable.

Let your actions speak.

Let your consistency build a reputation that outlasts your moods.

Because when everything else fails—discipline doesn't.

Stay consistent.

No matter the weather.

No matter who's watching.

No matter what the scoreboard says today.

Stay locked in.

And keep stacking days.

Chapter 16: Own Everything

Most people run from blame.

They point fingers.

Make excuses.

Blame their parents. Their past. The system. The weather.
Their ex. Their boss.

Anything but themselves.

But here's what I learned:

You don't grow until you take full ownership.

I've made mistakes.

Big ones.

Skipped school. Lied to my mom. Got expelled. Disrespected good people.

Nobody had to come fix it. That was on me.

And once I stopped trying to defend it, and just owned it, I got better.

That's where the shift happened.

In the Marine Corps, if you mess up, you pay for it.

No hiding.

If you're late, you pay.

If your gear isn't squared away, you pay.

If your attitude is trash, someone's going to check you fast.

It teaches you something real:

Your actions are your responsibility.

Nobody's coming to babysit you.

Nobody's going to walk behind you all day with a clipboard.

You either perform—or you answer for it.

That's life.

Now as a civilian, I still hold myself to that same standard.

If I don't get something done—it's not because I was "busy."

It's because I didn't prioritize it.

If I fall off track—it's not life's fault.

It's mine.

And that's not self-hate.

That's self-respect.

Because once you admit it's your fault—you also admit you can fix it.

Most people want to stay victims forever.

Because it's easier.

It gives them a story.

"I could've done more, but this happened."

They love that sentence.

It's the perfect excuse to stay stuck.

Not me.

I'm not afraid to say, "I messed up."

Because I follow it with, "I'll fix it."

That's power.

That's growth.

That's real life.

Accountability doesn't mean beating yourself up.

It means being honest with yourself.

About your habits.

Your effort.

Your attitude.

Your words.

If something's not working, don't complain about it—check yourself.

Then adjust. Then apply.

If you want to be respected, start with yourself.

Don't post about your goals. Show them.

Don't talk about discipline. Live it.

Don't say you're about it. Be about it.

Every day. Especially when nobody's watching.

Own your past.

Own your present.

Own your next move.

Even if it's hard.

Even if it hurts.

Because the moment you take full control?

That's the moment your whole life opens up.

Chapter 17: Seek the Hard Things

Most people avoid discomfort.

That's their first instinct—stay comfortable, stay safe, don't push too far, don't do too much.

But that's why they stay stuck.

That's why nothing changes.

I move the opposite way.

If it's uncomfortable, I lean into it.

If it's hard, I want to know why—and then I want to figure it out.

Because every hard thing I've ever gone through made me sharper.

Every tough moment built something in me.

And now?

I go looking for that feeling on purpose.

I'm not afraid of pain.

I've seen what real fear looks like. I've been hunted. I've had guns pointed at me. I've run until my legs gave out.

There's nothing in a classroom, a gym, or a job that scares me more than what I've already survived.

So I don't flinch anymore.

I lean in.

Goggins often talks about building mental toughness the same way you build physical strength—by putting yourself through pain and coming out stronger. That idea stuck with me.

That stuck with me.

Because it's true.

If you protect yourself from every hard thing, your mind stays soft.

And when life finally hits you?

You break.

But if you chase discomfort on purpose?

If you do hard things daily?

You get tough where it matters most—in your mind.

Goggins lives it.

That's why I look up to him.

It's not just the running or the pull-ups or the crazy challenges.

It's the mindset.

He doesn't wait to feel good.

He gets up and does the work no matter what.

That's how I move too.

Tired? Still go.

Busy? Make time.

Hurt? Heal while working.

Unmotivated? Doesn't matter.

Discipline over everything.

I don't do easy reps.

I don't do shortcuts.

I don't water things down just to say I finished.

If it's not testing me, I don't want it.

And when it gets uncomfortable, that's when I lock in harder.

Because I know growth is hiding inside that resistance.

I run toward the hard things now.

Wake up before I want to.

Train when it hurts.

Say no to distractions.

Say yes to the grind.

Even when no one else is doing it.

Especially then.

Because I don't want average.

I don't want normal.

I want real strength—built, not bought.

Goggins teaches the value of standing out even among the elite. That mindset pushed me to raise my own standard.

That line hit deep.

Because that's the target.

Not just to rise above the weak—but to keep rising even when surrounded by the strong.

No excuses.

No entitlement.

No soft talk.

Just daily discipline, in silence, while everyone else chases distractions.

You want to grow?

You want to be sharp?

Go do something hard on purpose.

And when it sucks?

Smile—and keep going.

That's how I move.

That's how real ones move.

Chapter 18: Don't Slow Down

Momentum is everything.

When you've been building, grinding, staying consistent—you don't stop just because things get "good."

You keep going.

You keep pressing forward.

Because the moment you ease up?

You lose the edge you worked so hard to earn.

I've seen what happens when people slow down too early.

They get comfortable.

They tell themselves they earned a break.

They let their routine slip, then their mindset follows.

And once that discipline breaks?

It's hard to get it back.

That's why I stay moving.

No matter how far I've come, I always act like I'm just getting started.

Because I am.

This isn't the finish line—it's just one checkpoint.

One class passed. One workout done. One chapter written.

Then it's on to the next.

People ask me, "When do you rest?"

I rest when it's earned.

Not when I feel like it.

Not because it's trending.

I rest with intention—not out of laziness.

Rest is part of the grind—but only after the work is done.

I keep a list.

Not just of goals—but of what I've already overcome.

I look at that list and remind myself:

You've been through worse.

You've handled more.

You're built for this.

So why slow down now?

Why coast when you were made to climb?

Success isn't about speed—it's about sustainability.

But sustainability doesn't mean soft.

It means being smart with your energy.

It means training consistently. Studying consistently. Building something solid.

It means finding your rhythm—and sticking to it, even on your worst days.

The world wants you to slow down.

Comfort wants you to take your foot off the gas.

Distractions want you to detour.

I say no.

Because if I stop now, I'd be disrespecting everything I've been through.

Every step, every scar, every lesson—it all brought me here.

And I won't throw it away just because the ride gets smooth for a minute.

I stay hungry.

I stay locked in.

And I keep the pressure on.

Because momentum is a weapon.

When you have it, you use it.

When you're winning—double down.

When you're focused—go harder.

When the fire's lit—don't let it go out.

Don't slow down.

Not when you're tired.

Not when you're ahead.

Not when they say "you've made it."

Because you haven't.

There's more work to do.

And I'm built to keep going.

Chapter 19: Know Your Worth

People will try to define you.

By your name.

Your background.

Your accent.

Your job title.

Your past mistakes.

They'll look at where you came from and decide how far you're allowed to go.

That's their problem—not mine.

I know who I am.

Because I earned it.

I didn't wake up with confidence.

I built it.

Through hard days. Through loss. Through long nights.

Through moments where no one saw the work but me.

You don't need permission to believe in yourself.

You don't need likes to confirm your vision.

You don't need approval to move forward.

Once you've put in the work?

You know what you're worth.

And you don't need to prove it to anyone.

I've been overlooked.

I've been doubted.

I've had people laugh in my face when I told them what I was working toward.

They assumed I'd stay small.

Stay stuck.

But I don't live by their limits.

I've already broken too many to care.

113

Self-worth isn't ego.

It's quiet.

It's the way you walk into a room without needing to be the loudest.

It's the way you carry yourself when no one's watching.

It's the way you handle pressure when it shows up uninvited.

Because if you never test yourself...

If you never push...

If you never go all-in...

Then how would you ever know what you're capable of?

My worth isn't in what I say.

It's in what I do.

Every class I pass. Every mile I run. Every time I show up when I could've made excuses.

That's where it's built.

And every time I stack another win—even a small one—it reminds me that I'm not done.

I'm just getting warmed up.

People will doubt you until the work is done.

Then they'll act like they knew all along.

Let them talk.

Let them sleep.

You keep building.

And when it's all said and done?

They'll realize you never needed them to believe in you.

You just needed you.

Know your worth.

Not just with words—but with work.

Walk like it.

Train like it.

Show up like it.

Every day.

Chapter 20: Run Your Race

Everyone's watching everyone else.

Scrolling. Judging. Comparing.

Looking at who's doing what, who got what, who's ahead, who's behind.

It's a trap.

And if you're not careful, it'll kill your focus.

I used to get caught up in it too.

Seeing other people graduate sooner. Make more money. Take different paths.

It made me question if I was behind.

But I wasn't.

I was just on my path—and that's all that matters.

Now I don't care what pace anyone else is moving at.

I stay in my lane.

I run my race.

Because comparison is a thief.

It steals your peace.

It distracts your focus.

It makes you forget how far you've already come.

I came from nothing.

I wasn't supposed to make it to high school, let alone college.

Wasn't supposed to be walking into classrooms, training for a career in healthcare, writing a damn book while doing it.

So I don't care who's ahead of me.

I just care that I'm still moving.

You never know what someone else is really dealing with.

Social media shows the highlight reel.

But real life is messy.

It's slow.

It's hard.

It's not always pretty—and that's fine.

That's real growth.

That's the mindset.

Stop checking the scoreboard.

Stop watching the next man's steps.

Turn that energy inward.

Be better than you were yesterday.

That's the only race that matters.

I measure my progress by effort.

Not by trophies.

Not by who's clapping.

I know when I gave 100%. I know when I coasted. I know when I slacked.

So I hold myself accountable—and keep it moving.

It's not about being the fastest.

It's about not quitting.

It's about showing up when you don't feel like it.

It's about knowing this path is yours—and nobody else gets to define it.

Let them watch.

Let them talk.

Let them flash their wins.

You stay locked in.

Head down. Eyes forward.

Run your race.

Chapter 21: Be the Example

Like it or not—people are watching you.

Your younger siblings.

Your classmates.

Your friends.

The ones who talk trash, and the ones who secretly admire how you move.

They see you show up.

They see you grind.

They see how you react when things don't go your way.

They're watching.

That's pressure.

But pressure isn't a bad thing.

Pressure means you're in position.

You're not just surviving anymore—you're being looked at as a leader.

Not because you asked for it.

But because you earned it.

When I walk into a classroom, I carry a different energy.

Not because I think I'm better.

But because I know what I've been through to get here.

So I don't play around.

I don't waste time.

And whether people say it or not—they notice.

Leadership doesn't mean you're always the loudest.

It means you're the most reliable.

It means you move with consistency, discipline, and calm—
even when everything else is chaos.

It means when someone else is slipping, you don't lecture—
you show.

By how you carry yourself.

By how you work.

By how you don't break.

People come to me for advice now.

They ask me how I stay focused, how I keep showing up,
how I keep the energy right.

I don't give them motivational speeches.

I just tell the truth.

You either want it or you don't.

You either get up or you stay stuck.

That's it.

But what I do give them—without saying a word—is an example.

Someone who's been through real struggle.

Someone who's walked through fire and didn't flinch.

Someone who didn't make excuses, didn't cry for attention, didn't settle.

Someone who took every hard day—and used it.

A place in your mind where you store every tough moment you got through.

Because later, when life hits again, you reach into that cabinet.

You remember who you are.

You remember what you've done.

And you realize—you're still standing.

That's leadership.

That's self-respect.

Being the example doesn't mean you're perfect.

It means you're real.

You show people what it looks like to keep pushing—even with scars, even with setbacks, even with doubts.

You don't quit.

You adjust. You rise.

And you let the work speak.

Be the example.

Not for praise.

Not for likes.

But because you've become the person you needed back when you were still figuring it out.

Now it's your turn to lead.

Silently.

Consistently.

Fully.

Chapter 22: What I Leave Behind

When it's all said and done, I'm not trying to be remembered for being flashy.

I'm not chasing clout.

I don't care about being famous.

I care about being solid.

The real ones don't leave behind distraction—they leave behind impact.

Not just what they said—but how they moved.

Not what they posted—but how they lived.

I want to be known as someone who never gave up.

Someone who didn't back down when life got messy.

Someone who didn't need perfect conditions to stay locked in.

Someone who came from struggle, owned it, and still chose to rise.

I'm not doing this just for now.

I'm doing this for what comes after.

For the version of me that'll one day look back and be proud.

And for anyone who feels like they're too far behind, too broken, too unheard to become something better.

If someone ever asks what kind of man I was, I want the answer to be simple:

"He didn't make excuses. He handled his business. He stayed real."

That's it.

No drama. No act. Just consistency and purpose.

I've already broken cycles.

I've already passed points where most people quit.

So now I'm focused on building something that lasts.

My education. My health. My mindset. My peace.

That's legacy.

I used to think legacy was about what you leave behind for people.

Now I know it's about what you build in yourself—and how it helps others rise, even when you're not in the room.

Your words. Your example. Your energy.

If that leaves someone better than it found them—you've done your job.

That conversation decides everything.

It shapes your habits. Your decisions. Your future.

And when you win that inner war, the outside world can't touch you.

If I ever have a family of my own, I want my daughter to look at this book and say,
 "Damn… that's my dad."

I want my son to look at my life and say,
 "I want to be like my father one day."

If I leave one message behind for them, it's this:

Stay true to yourself.

Forget what people think.

Do what makes you happy.

Your father was never the one who gave up.

As my daughter, I want you to carry that same fire.

You better be on TV as an Olympic champion.

Never let anyone kill your fire.

LET IT BLAZE.

Legacy isn't a moment.

It's what you do daily.

It's who you become when no one's watching.

It's how you move when no one's clapping.

That's what I'm leaving behind:

Discipline. Drive. Truth. No shortcuts.

Only proof.

Chapter 23: Believe Anyway

There were a lot of times I shouldn't have believed in myself.

The odds were stacked.

The room was against me.

The path wasn't clear.

But I believed anyway.

Because deep down, I knew what I carried inside couldn't be measured by outside opinions.

I wasn't supposed to make it out of where I started.

I wasn't supposed to learn English, get through school, join the Marines, earn respect, become a student again, write a book.

But here I am.

And it didn't happen because I had perfect timing or perfect support.

It happened because I chose not to quit.

Even when I had every reason to.

Belief is a choice.

A mindset.

You either believe in your potential—or you stay small because it's safer.

You either trust the grind—or you spend your life doubting every move.

I chose belief.

Even when I didn't feel ready.

Even when I didn't have proof yet.

I believed in what I was becoming.

That belief kept me in motion.

When I got rejected—I kept going.

When I failed—I learned and tried again.

When people doubted me—I locked in even more.

When I didn't have applause—I clapped for myself.

Because if you don't believe in your own mission, nobody else will.

You want to build something?

You better believe in it when no one else does.

You want to change your life?

You better believe it's possible before it happens.

Belief doesn't come after the win—it comes before.

You don't get confidence from talking about it.

You get it from walking through fire and not breaking.

You build belief by surviving days that were meant to break you—and waking up the next day still hungry.

The way I see it?

If you've made it this far—you're not average.

You're not soft.

You're not hopeless.

You're just one decision away from becoming who you were born to be.

So no matter what's going on in your life…

No matter who walked away…

No matter how far behind you feel…

Believe anyway.

Not blindly.

But boldly.

With proof. With effort. With action.

Believe with your work.

Believe with your habits.

Believe with your discipline.

You've already made it through storms most people couldn't handle.

Don't doubt now.

This is where it gets real.

And if nobody else tells you this—I believe in you.

Now it's your turn.

Believe in you.

And move like it.

Chapter 24: It Takes Time

Everybody wants results right now.

Fast success. Fast growth. Fast rewards.

But that's not how real things are built.

Especially not when you come from nothing.

When the world didn't hand you a shortcut, a connection, or a clean starting line.

For people like us?

It takes time.

And that's okay.

Because we're not just trying to get their fast—we're trying to build something solid.

And solid takes time.

There were moments I felt stuck.

Like all the work I was doing wasn't showing up yet.

Like everyone else was moving ahead while I was still grinding in silence.

But every time I felt that frustration rise up, I reminded myself:

Keep working.

Even when it's slow.

Even when it's quiet.

Even when it feels like no one's watching.

Progress isn't always loud.

Sometimes it's invisible.

It's in the early mornings where you don't skip.

It's in the hours you study while everyone else is out.

It's in the discipline you show when nobody else is doing it.

Those moments add up.

I didn't get here overnight.

Nobody handed me a blueprint.

I had to figure it out, mess up, adjust, and keep going.

And I'm still doing that now.

Still learning. Still building. Still sharpening.

Because their's always more to do—and I'm not in a rush.

David Goggins, He says, "When you think you're done, you're only at 40%."

That's truth.

Most people quit because the payoff isn't fast enough.

But the strong?

They stay in it.

Because they know it's coming—if they don't stop.

One brick at a time.

I don't skip steps.

I don't chase hype.

I don't need everything to happen today.

I just need to get better today.

If you're reading this and you're tired of waiting on results?

Keep going.

You're not behind.

You're not failing.

You're just still in it—and that's exactly where you're supposed to be.

The ones who win long-term?

They're not always the loudest, fastest, or most followed.

They're the ones who didn't quit when it got slow.

They're the ones who stayed locked in when it wasn't glamorous.

They're the ones who respected the process—even when it was silent.

It takes time.

But that's what makes it real.

That's what makes it worth it.

And when it hits?

It'll hit different—because you earned every inch.

Chapter 25: I'm Not the Same

If you knew me back then—and you're looking at me now?

Just know you're not looking at the same man.

Not even close.

I've changed.

Not for attention.

Not to impress anyone.

But in the ways that actually matter.

How I handle stress.

How I manage my time.

How I respond to setbacks.

How I treat people.

How I talk to myself.

There were times in my life where I reacted to everything.

Someone doubted me—I got loud.

Something didn't go my way—I gave up.

I was always on edge.

Always defensive.

Always unsure of who I was.

That's not me anymore.

Now, I move calm.

I move with purpose.

I don't have to prove anything.

I let my consistency do the talking.

I let my presence speak for itself.

I'm not perfect.

But I'm disciplined.

I don't chase motivation.

I chase structure.

I don't follow trends.

I follow my plan.

Growth isn't about changing how you look.

It's about changing how you move.

It's when the stuff that used to throw you off doesn't even rattle you anymore.

It's when you stop needing to defend yourself—and you just stay focused.

It's when you stop reacting—and start responding.

That's growth.

Because that's what flipped everything for me.

I got tired of being the guy with potential but no direction.

Tired of saying, "One day."

Tired of surviving instead of building.

So I changed.

And the wild thing?

A lot of people won't even recognize the new version of you.

They'll try to treat you like the old you.

They'll talk to you like you're still stuck.

Like you still think small.

Like you still need their approval.

Let them.

You don't owe anyone the same version of you forever.

Especially when that version was built for survival—not success.

You outgrew it.

You evolved.

You leveled up.

You're not that person anymore—and that's the point.

So if you're reading this, wondering if it's okay to grow past your environment?

Let me tell you:

It is.

Outgrow the limits.

Outgrow the habits.

Outgrow the people, if you need to.

Just don't shrink to make them comfortable.

I'm not the same.

And I'm proud of that.

Because every version of me had a purpose—but this one?

This version?

Is built to lead.

Chapter 26: Be the One They Can Count On

Most people break under pressure.

They quit the moment things feel uncomfortable.

They disappear when you need them most.

I've seen it too many times.

That's why I became the opposite.

I made a decision a long time ago:

Be the one they can count on.

Not just when it's easy.

Not just when it's convenient.

But when it's late. When it's hard. When it's silent.

When most people disappear—that's when I show up.

You don't need attention to be dependable.

You just need to be consistent.

You don't need to say yes to everything.

You just need to keep your word.

When you say you'll do something—do it.

When you say you'll be their—be their.

And if you can't—say it straight.

No lies. No cover-ups. No weak energy.

Just honesty and reliability.

I didn't grow up with a safety net.

I learned early that not everyone shows up when they say they will.

And I promised myself I wouldn't be like that.

I would be the one who doesn't flinch when it gets hard.

The one who answers the phone when others ignore it.

The one who stands tall when things go left.

It's not about being perfect.

It's about being present.

Being solid.

Being that calm in the storm when everyone else is panicking.

That applies to being dependable too.

You don't have to know everything.

You just have to show up.

Every time.

People don't remember hype.

They remember who held them down when life got dark.

They remember who kept it real when things got messy.

They remember who showed up—not with answers, but with presence.

So if someone needs me?

I'm their.

Not because I want credit.

But because I know what it feels like to be on your own.

I know what it's like to wish someone would just say,
"I got you."

Now I get to be that voice.

And the best part?

I didn't have to be born that way.

I built it.

Through routine.

Through experience.

Through showing up for myself first.

Because when you're solid within, you can finally be solid for others.

Be the one they can count on.

In silence.

In struggle.

In the everyday.

Because their's power in being the most dependable one in the room.

And trust me—people never forget, it.

Chapter 27: Peace Isn't Given, It's Earned

Peace doesn't come from having a perfect life.

It doesn't come from a fat paycheck, a smooth schedule, or a comfortable bed.

Real peace?

It's earned.

You don't get peace by avoiding the hard stuff.

You get peace by facing it.

By doing what needs to be done.

By keeping your word.

By handling your business without needing to tell everyone you're doing it.

I used to think peace was something that came later.

After I had enough money.

After I finished school.

After I proved myself.

But now I know—that mindset keeps you chasing forever.

Peace starts the moment you get real with yourself.

The moment you stop running.

My peace comes from knowing I gave everything I had today.

That I trained when I didn't feel like it.

That I kept my word even when nobody was watching.

That I handled my responsibilities and didn't make excuses.

That I stayed true to my values, even when no one clapped for it.

There's a different kind of sleep that hits when you know you earned your rest.

No guilt. No second-guessing.

Just silence and stillness.

That's peace.

And I take that seriously.

Because when I lay down at night, it's just me and that mirror.

No social media.

No distractions.

Just me.

And I need to know I lived like someone who's locked in.

Someone who doesn't quit.

Someone who doesn't fake it.

People chase peace by avoiding problems.

I chase peace by solving them.

By showing up.

By staying uncomfortable enough to grow—but solid enough
to breathe.

I'm not perfect.

But I'm proud of who I'm becoming.

Because every day I get a little more focused.

A little more honest.

A little more free.

You don't find peace.

You build it.

You earn it.

One decision at a time.

Chapter 28: Alone, Not Lonely

There's a difference between being alone—and being lonely.

Most people don't know the difference.

They panic when they're by themselves.

They fill the silence with distractions.

TV. Music. Distractions. People who don't even add value.

Because they're afraid to sit with their own thoughts.

I'm not.

I've grown to respect the quiet.

Because that's where the real work happens.

That's where clarity shows up.

That's where I hear my own voice without the echo of everyone else's opinions.

Solitude sharpened me.

It made me more focused.

More intentional.

More real.

I don't need a crowd to feel solid.

I don't need group chats to feel seen.

I don't need approval to feel worthy.

When I'm alone, I think better.

I move smarter.

I remember why I started.

That's when I check myself.

Am I still on point?

Am I doing what I said I would?

Am I slipping?

That accountability hits different when there's no one around to blame.

People ask me how I stay focused.

I tell them straight:

Learn how to be alone without losing your grip.

Because if you need distraction to stay sane, you're not stable—you're weak.

If you need constant attention, you haven't built your own confidence yet.

And if you can't sit in a room by yourself and feel peace?

You've got work to do.

I've sat in silence with nothing but my thoughts.

I've walked through rooms where nobody clapped.

I've done the work with no one around to validate it.

And I came out stronger.

Cleaner.

Louder in presence—not in volume.

So yeah, I move alone a lot.

Not because I don't have people who care.

But because I know my best work happens when it's just me and the goal.

No distractions.

No distractions.

Just vision and action.

Alone, not lonely.

And that's exactly where I need to be.

Chapter 29: You Don't Have to Prove Anything

I used to carry that weight on my back.

The need to prove myself.

To show people I belonged.

To show I was worth something.

To prove I wasn't soft.

That I wasn't a quitter.

That I wasn't just another face in the crowd.

But here's what I learned:

You don't have to prove anything to anyone.

Especially not to people who weren't in the room when you were struggling.

The only one I need to prove anything to—is me.

And I do that every day.

By staying consistent.

By holding myself accountable.

By waking up and moving like someone who has goals—not just dreams.

People will doubt you no matter what.

Even when you do everything right.

Even when you rise.

They'll still talk.

Still throw shade.

Still act like your success is luck.

Let them.

Because the minute you start living to impress people—you start drifting from your purpose.

I don't chase applause anymore.

I chase alignment.

Is what I'm doing aligned with my values?

My discipline?

My future?

If the answer's yes—I move. Quietly. Consistently.

That's how I live now.

Not for validation.

But for completion.

For growth.

For self-respect.

I didn't come this far just to win people over.

I came this far to win myself over.

To become someone I'm proud of.

To become the version of me that can't be shaken by outside distraction.

You want to know how to quiet the world?

Start moving like you don't need its permission.

Start moving like your mission is bigger than their opinions.

Start living like you know who you are, with or without their likes.

You don't have to prove anything.

Not to the ones who left.

Not to the ones who doubted you.

Not even to the ones who cheered you on.

You just have to stay true.

Stay locked in.

Stay you.

Chapter 30: Remember, Don't Return

You can't grow if you're always running from your past.

And you can't move forward if you're always stuck in it either.

You've got to find the balance.

Respect where you came from—but don't live their.

I remember the pain.

I remember the hunger, the pressure, the fear.

I remember the silence, the waiting, the moments I thought it was over.

I don't try to erase those things.

They made me.

They shaped my instincts, my drive, my focus.

But I don't live their anymore.

I don't carry it like a wound.

I carry it like a weapon.

Because the version of me that came through that?

That's a strong man.

Not a victim.

Not a product of circumstance.

A product of choice.

You've got to be careful with the past.

It can trap you in two ways:

You run from it so hard, you lose who you are.

You hold onto it so tight, you stop evolving.

I don't do either.

I look back to remind myself what I've survived—not to relive it.

I've had people try to bring up my past like it's a weakness.

Like it disqualifies me from being great.

What they don't understand?

That past is the reason I'm great.

I earned everything through fire.

Nothing was handed to me.

Nothing was easy.

That's why I don't break now.

And some of the hardest ones are about your past.

But once you own it?

Once you say, "Yeah, that happened—and I'm still standing"?

You take the power back.

So no, I don't run from my past.

I use it.

I learn from it.

But I don't live in it.

The mission now?

Keep growing.

Keep evolving.

Keep building a life that makes the past proud—but doesn't repeat it.

Remember where you came from.

But don't return to who you used to be.

You've come too far.

Chapter 31: Outgrowing People Is Normal

This part's not easy.

But it's real.

When you start pushing forward—not everyone comes with you.

And they're not supposed to.

You'll start to notice the change.

The conversations feel different.

The energy starts to shift.

You're focused—they're distracted.

You're building—they're complaining.

You're growing—they're comfortable.

At first, you try to bring them with you.

Put them on game.

Share the mindset.

Share the vision.

But eventually, you realize:

They don't want it like you do.

And that hurts.

Especially when it's people you've known for years.

People who were there during your low points.

But here's the truth:

Loyalty to your future is more important than loyalty to your comfort zone.

You can love people and still outgrow them.

You can wish them well—and still move without them.

You can support from a distance.

But you don't hold back just to stay close.

I've had to walk away from circles that stopped moving forward.

Not out of ego.

Out of necessity.

Because if I stay too long in a place that doesn't challenge me—I become one of them.

And that's not an option.

But some people stopped a long time ago.

They're just existing now.

Waiting on weekends, wasting time, wondering why nothing's changing.

I couldn't do that.

I'd rather walk alone with momentum than stand still in a crowd.

When you grow, your standards rise.

Your discipline sharpens.

Your focus narrows.

And not everyone wants to adjust to that.

Let them go.

Not out of hate—but out of respect for your own mission.

If someone's meant to grow with you, they will.

But if they don't?

Let that chapter close.

Keep writing yours.

Keep moving.

Keep rising.

Outgrowing people doesn't make you cold.

It makes you aware.

And that awareness?

It'll take you places comfort never could.

Chapter 32: Raise Your Standard

Every time you settle, you teach yourself that it's okay.

Every time you skip what you said you'd do, you lower the bar.

Every time you accept less from yourself, you lose a piece of who you're trying to become.

It doesn't start with big failures.

It starts small.

Sleeping in "just this once."

Skipping a workout because you're tired.

Hanging around people who drain you.

Laughing at stuff that doesn't align with your values.

Letting your old self creep back in through the cracks.

That's how standards slip.

One choice at a time.

I had to catch myself.

I used to say I was "disciplined."

But my actions weren't always lining up.

And that gap?

That's where self-respect lives—or dies.

So I raised the standard.

I stopped letting myself slide with weak excuses.

I stopped calling it a "bad day" when I really just lacked structure.

I stopped being okay with just enough.

Now I ask myself straight:

Would the man I'm becoming be proud of how I handled today?

If not—fix it.

No emotion. Just correction.

People think raising your standard is about being better than others.

It's not.

It's about being better than your old self.

It's about not letting the upgraded version of you be built on a shaky foundation.

My own personal standard.

No skipping.

No flinching.

No coasting.

Even when nobody sees it.

Especially then.

Your standard is your blueprint.

It's how you show up when no one's holding you accountable.

It's how you carry yourself when you don't feel motivated.

It's how you move when pressure shows up.

Every time you raise it—your life changes with it.

You stop attracting distractions.

You stop entertaining nonsense.

You stop tolerating less than you deserve.

Raise your standard—and protect it.

Because the second you let it drop?

So does everything else.

Chapter 33: Move With Intention

You can't afford to move like your time doesn't matter.

You can't afford to keep reacting to life like you don't have a say.

Because you do.

And every move you make—counts.

Intentional living isn't about being perfect.

It's about being aware.

Knowing why you're doing what you're doing.

171

And making sure it lines up with where you say you want to go.

When I wake up, I don't just "see what happens."

I have a plan.

I move with structure.

If it's not pushing me forward—I cut it.

If it's draining my focus—I remove it.

If it's a habit that keeps me stuck—I change it.

That's how I protect my momentum.

I used to go through days just reacting.

Someone texts me—I stop what I'm doing.

Something distracts me—I lean into it.

I'd waste hours doing things that brought me nothing.

Not growth. Not peace. Not purpose.

Just distraction.

That's not how I move anymore.

Now, everything I do runs through a filter:

Does this align with who I'm becoming?

If not—why am I doing it?

I don't go to the gym just to post about it.

I go to train my mind and body.

I don't go to class just to pass.

I go to become dangerous in my field.

I don't read books just to say I read them.

I study. Apply. Evolve.

That's the difference.

You can't keep saying you want more while living on autopilot.

You either take control of your time—or the world will waste it for you.

Move with intention.

Talk with intention.

Rest with intention.

Be around people who match that energy—or distance yourself with intention too.

You've got one life.

Make every move mean something.

Chapter 34: It's All On You

Nobody's coming.

Nobody's going to wake you up.

Nobody's going to hand you discipline.

Nobody's going to force you to study, to train, to evolve.

That's on you.

Your future?

On you.

Your mental health?

On you.

The way you respond when life hits?

Still you.

You can blame the past.

You can blame your family.

You can blame the system, the school, the weather, the world.

But none of that changes the fact that you're the one who has to do something about it.

There's freedom in that.

Not fear—freedom.

Because once you stop blaming, you start building.

You stop reacting, and you start responding.

You stop waiting, and you start creating.

I had to learn this the hard way.

I used to wait.

Wait for the right moment.

Wait for someone to guide me.

Wait for a better environment.

But guess what?

The "right time" never came.

The only thing that changed was me.

I took control of my habits.

My energy.

My environment.

My circle.

My mindset.

And that's when things started moving.

Not before.

Because it reminds me that ownership isn't a one-time
decision—it's daily.

Every day you wake up, you've got a choice:

Own it—or avoid it.

Take action—or take the easy way out.

Build yourself—or blame someone else.

When things go wrong, I don't look for someone to point at.

I ask:

Where did I go soft?

Where did I slip?

What do I need to fix?

And then I fix it.

That's ownership.

You want power?

Take responsibility.

You want peace?

Stop outsourcing your control.

You want results?

Hold yourself accountable before anyone else can.

It's all on you.

And that's not pressure.

That's permission.

To take back your life.

To take back your time.

To become the version of yourself you were meant to be.

Chapter 35: Do It Anyway

Discipline doesn't ask how you feel.

It doesn't check your mood.

It doesn't care if you're tired, sad, frustrated, or unmotivated.

It just asks: Did you show up?

Some days you'll wake up energized.

Other days you'll feel like staying under the blanket forever.

But the disciplined ones?

They do it anyway.

The workout still gets done.

The studying still happens.

The grind continues—even when the emotions don't match the mission.

Because once you let feelings lead—you'll start falling off.

You'll skip once.

Then again.

And before you know it, you're back at square one wondering what happened.

It wasn't a big failure.

It was all those little decisions where you chose comfort over consistency.

When I stopped making excuses, I started seeing the results.

I remember being so tired, completely overwhelmed with assignments. I had a chemistry lab project that took hours just to complete the report—every detail had to be right. On top of that, I had physics problems due the same night. Most people would've tapped out. But I laughed and told myself,

"This is easy." You know what? On top of my full schedule, I decided I'd write six more chapters for my book that night. No excuses. Just put on the grind.

Feel tired? Still show up.

Don't want to study? Open the book anyway.

Don't feel "inspired"? Do the work anyway.

Because momentum doesn't come from motivation—it comes from motion.

From doing the thing you said you'd do.

This mindset changed everything for me.

I stopped negotiating with weakness.

I stopped letting how I felt dictate how I moved.

And when I did that?

I became unstoppable.

People say, "Listen to your body."

I say, "Train your mind."

Because most of the time, your body is fine—your thoughts are the problem.

You tell yourself you can't, and so you don't.

You talk yourself out of greatness, out of growth, out of progress.

So now I keep it simple:

Feelings don't drive me.

Discipline does.

Structure does.

Purpose does.

And that shows up—even when I don't feel like it.

You want to separate yourself?

Start doing the work when nobody would blame you for skipping.

Start showing up on the days you'd usually disappear.

Start pushing when it's cold, when you're sore, when you're doubting everything.

That's the difference.

Anyone can be consistent when it's easy.

But the ones who go far?

They do it anyway.

Chapter 36: Start Now

There's always a reason to wait.

"I'm tired."

"I'm not ready."

"I'll start next week."

"I'll just do it tomorrow."

That's the trap.

And that trap has ruined more dreams than failure ever could.

The longer you wait, the heavier the start becomes.

You build it up in your head.

You talk yourself out of it.

And suddenly the thing you were supposed to do today?

It turns into next month.

Then next year.

Then never.

People love to say they're "waiting for the right time."

But here's the truth:

There is no right time.

There's only now.

When I started building discipline, I didn't feel ready.

When I joined the Marine Corps, I wasn't fully ready.

When I stepped into college, chasing a new career—I wasn't ready.

I just started anyway.

And figured it out on the way.

You don't need a perfect plan.

You need action.

You don't need all the answers.

You need movement.

You don't need permission.

You need to take control.

You don't wait for perfect conditions—you build under pressure.

You start where you are.

You start with what you have.

You start, even if your hands are shaking.

Waiting is easy.

Starting is hard.

But once you start?

You shift everything.

Your energy.

Your confidence.

Your belief.

And even if you're not where you want to be yet?

At least you're moving.

At least you're in motion.

At least you're not stuck watching from the sidelines anymore.

Whatever you've been thinking about doing?

Start now.

Not tomorrow.

Not when you feel better.

Right now.

Because this version of you?

The one who's reading this, feeling that pull to act?

That version is ready enough.

Chapter 37: Stay Hungry

Getting started is one thing.

Staying locked in after the pressure fades?

That's different.

That's what separates the focused from the finished.

Most people only move when their back's against the wall.

They only grind when it's uncomfortable.

Only pray when things fall apart.

Only focus when the fire's hot.

But once things calm down?

They cool off too.

They lose the edge that got them there.

I made a decision:

Never get too comfortable.

I don't wait for pain to wake me up.

I stay ready.

Because the moment you stop pushing?

You start slipping.

Success is a setup if you stop moving after you taste it.

It makes you soft.

Makes you forget who you were when you were fighting to get out.

Makes you forget how far you've come—and how far their still is to go.

Complacency doesn't announce itself.

It shows up quietly.

In the skipped reps.

In the snoozed alarm.

In the half-effort work.

In the, "I'll do it later."

I remind myself daily:

You're not done.

You're not finished.

You're not above the work.

I don't train just to maintain—I train to dominate.

I don't study just to pass—I study to prepare for the next level.

I don't wake up just to go through the motions—I wake up to get sharper.

Hunger doesn't mean being dissatisfied with your life.

It means respecting your potential enough to never settle.

The minute you stop chasing something higher?

You stop growing.

So I stay hungry.

Even when things are good.

Especially when things are good.

Because that's when most people stop—and I refuse to be most people.

Comfort is where purpose goes to die.

Stay uncomfortable.

Stay alert.

Stay hungry.

Chapter 38: Nobody claps at the start

When you first start building something real, it's quiet.

Nobody notices.

Nobody claps.

Nobody says "good job."

It's just you, your vision, and a whole lot of silence.

At first, you think people will support you just because you started.

But they don't.

You'll drop your first idea, your first rep, your first step—and all you'll hear is doubt, or worse... nothing.

And that's exactly when most people quit.

But I didn't.

Because I wasn't building for claps—I was building for change.

In the beginning, no one believed in my goals like I did.

They didn't see the point.

They didn't understand why I'd wake up early, why I'd train when no one was watching, why I'd say no to distractions just to sit and study or write or grow.

Because to them, I was just "doing too much."

But to me, I was just getting started.

You have to be okay with being unseen for a while.

You have to be okay with not being praised.

Because greatness doesn't come with applause in the early rounds.

It comes with sweat, repetition, and silence.

I don't need approval.

I don't need attention.

I just need my goals, my plan, and my work ethic.

That's the combo.

Let them sleep.

Let them laugh.

Let them scroll past your progress.

When it's time, they'll see what you were doing while they were talking.

Because here's the truth:

Nobody claps at the start.

But when you stay consistent?

They'll try to act like they believed in you the whole time.

Let them clap later.

You?
You build now.

Chapter 39: I Remember What It Was Like

I don't forget.

I don't forget the nights I went to bed hungry.

I don't forget the fear of not knowing what tomorrow would bring.

I don't forget watching my parents stretch everything they had just to keep us going.

And that's why I don't complain now.

That's why I don't quit when it gets hard.

Because I've already lived through worse.

When life starts getting comfortable, people soften up.

They stop grinding.

They stop appreciating.

They lose the urgency that built them.

Not me.

Because I remember what it was like to have nothing.

I remember sharing everything.

I remember wearing shoes that didn't fit.

I remember hearing "we can't afford that" over and over.

And I carry that with me—not as pain, but as power.

All the past struggles.

All the moments you survived.

Remind yourself who you are.

Remind yourself what you've already overcome.

Remind yourself you don't quit.

I'm grateful for what I have now.

But I'll never get complacent.

Because I know what it took to get here.

That memory?

It keeps me sharp.

It keeps me grounded.

It keeps me hungry.

So yeah, I work hard.

I move different.

I stay disciplined.

Because I've seen the bottom—and I'm not going back.

I remember what it was like.
And I use that memory to push forward every day.

Chapter 40: Grateful, But Not Finished

I look around sometimes and think—"Man... I made it
further than I ever thought I would."

And I mean that.

I'm not where I used to be.

I'm not struggling like I was.

I've got peace now.
Structure.
A purpose that's real.

But just because I'm grateful, doesn't mean I'm done.

Most people hit a milestone and ease up.

They think they've arrived.

They stop pushing because life isn't painful anymore.

But I didn't start this to coast—I started this to become something greater.

Gratitude isn't the finish line.
It's fuel.

It reminds me that everything I prayed for, I now wake up and grind inside of.

So I don't take that lightly.

I use it.

I'm thankful for the struggle because it made me focused.

I'm thankful for the slow days because they taught me patience.

I'm thankful for the pressure because it shaped my mindset.

But I'm not done yet.

You raise the standard.

You double down.

That's how I live.

Grateful for today.

Locked in for tomorrow.

No resting on what I've already done—because I know what's still possible.

I look in the mirror and I see progress.

But I also see more work.

More discipline.

More sharpening to do.

More people I can inspire—by how I move, not just what I say.

So yeah, I'm proud.

But I'm not satisfied.

I've got more to write.

More to build.

More to prove—to myself.

Grateful, but not finished.

That's the mindset.

Chapter 41: You're Not Late

The world moves fast.

People love to remind you how far ahead someone else is.

"By 25 you should have this."

"By 30 you should be here."

"Why aren't you doing what they're doing?"

Let me say it straight:

You're not late.

Everyone's clock is different.

Some people peak early.

Some people peak late.

Some take off fast.

Some build in silence for years before anyone notices.

All of it is valid.

All of it is real.

I used to think I was behind.

Watching people graduate before me.

Start families before me.

Make more money, get more recognition, post more wins.

But I had to check myself:

Are they living my life?
Are they carrying my story?
Did they come from where I came from?

No.

So their pace isn't mine.

When you're locked in?

You can become one of the most driven people alive.

Once you take control, your past doesn't matter anymore.

Only your actions now do.

So if you're still figuring it out?

If you're building in silence?

If you're not where you want to be yet?

Good.

It means you're still in motion.

It means you still have time to shift.

You're not late.

You're just early in the process.

And the people who laugh now?

They'll watch in silence later.

Don't rush greatness.

Don't compare timelines.

Just stay consistent.

Every day you put in the work, you're closing the gap.

On your time.

In your way.

With no apology.

You're not late.
 You're just not finished yet.

Chapter 42: No More Excuses

Everybody's got a reason.

Too tired.
 Too busy.

Too late.

Too early.

Too much going on.

Not enough time.

Not enough support.

Excuses sound smart when you say them.

But they don't build anything.

You know what does?

Ownership.

I've used excuses before.

I've told myself,
  "Today's not the day."
  "I'll start after this."
  "I'm not ready yet."

And every time I did that?

Nothing changed.

The day everything shifted for me was the day I stopped looking for reasons—and started taking action.

No matter the situation.

No matter the pressure.

I told myself,
"Figure it out anyway."

You can't move forward and make excuses at the same time.

One has to die.

That's real.

Because most of the time, it's not the world stopping you.

It's you.

Your fear.
 Your comfort.
 Your hesitation.

So I had to get out of my own way.

And that meant no more blaming.

No more waiting for someone to come save me.

No more letting my situation define my output.

You're not always going to feel like it.
 You're not always going to have the ideal conditions.

But the work still has to get done.

The training still has to happen.
 The growth still has to be pursued.
 The habits still have to be built.

With or without perfect circumstances.

Excuses don't care about your goals.

And your goals don't care about your excuses.

If you want results?

Let the excuses go.

Start where you are.

With what you have.

And do what needs to be done.

No more excuses.

Only effort.

Chapter 43: You've Always Had It

The more you grow, the more you realize—you didn't need more motivation.

You didn't need a better schedule.

You didn't need permission.

You just needed to believe in what was already inside you.

Everything I needed?

I had it the whole time.

The strength.

The discipline.

The fire.

The clarity.

The hunger.

It was buried under self-doubt, comfort, and distraction.

Once I cut that stuff off?

It all came out.

People think they need some outside breakthrough.

But the truth is?

Most people are sitting on everything they need—they just never get focused enough to tap into it.

I used to think I was missing something.

That I had to wait until I was "ready."

But the moment I started taking real ownership?

I saw it.

I already had the focus—I just wasn't using it.

I already had the work ethic—I just wasn't applying it.

I already had the mindset—I just wasn't trusting it.

Now I move different.

Because I know I'm not lacking.

I'm just unlocking.

Every time I choose discipline over comfort, I unlock more of who I am.

Every time I finish what I said I would, I become stronger.

Every time I hold the line when it's hard, I grow.

You've got it in you too.

All of it.

You're not broken.

You're not too late.

You're not underqualified.

You're just not finished.

The version of you that changes everything?

Is already in their.

You just have to put in the reps to bring it out.

You've always had it.

Now prove it.

Chapter 44: Okay to be Misunderstood

You can't control others' opinions, so sometimes you just have to let them misunderstand you.

You're going to lose people when you zero in.

They won't get why you're distant.

Why you don't go out anymore.

Why you stopped replying fast.

Why your energy is different.

Let them.

They'll say:

"You've changed."
"You're acting brand new."
"You're too serious."

And they're right.

Because you did change.

You stopped entertaining distractions.

You stopped giving energy to things that weren't building your future.

You stopped explaining yourself to people who aren't living with your discipline.

That's not being fake.

That's being focused.

When you raise your standards, you automatically become "too much" for people who refuse to grow.

Let them fall off.

Let them assume.

Let them run their mouth.

You don't need to convince them of anything.

And when you choose to step out of that comfort?

People will try to pull you back.

Ignore it.

Let them talk.

Let them misunderstand.

You're not here to be understood.
You're here to become something they never saw coming.

You don't owe explanations for being focused.

You don't owe comfort to people who stayed the same.

You owe everything to the version of you that decided to go all in.

So when people start to distance themselves?

Wish them peace—and keep grinding.

When they say you're "doing too much"?

Smile and get back to work.

They don't need to get it.

They'll understand later.

Let them misunderstand you.

Your results will do the explaining.

Chapter 45: Don't Lose Your Rhythm

Once you find your groove—protect it.

When your routine is solid, when your discipline's high, when your habits are dialed in?

That's the most dangerous version of you.

And that's when the distractions show up the loudest.

They don't hit when you're weak.

They hit when you're finally moving right.

That's when people come around with "just this once" energy.

That's when your old habits try to creep back in.

That's when the distraction shows up.

It's not random.

It's resistance.

And if you don't catch it?

You'll lose your rhythm.

You'll miss one workout.

Then two.

You'll slip on your bedtime.

You'll scroll a little longer.

You'll eat something that slows you down.

And before you know it?

You're back at the bottom wondering what happened.

I don't let that happen anymore.

Because I know what it took to get here.

And I'm not throwing that away for a cheap dopamine hit.

The rhythm is sacred.

If you lose it—it's hell to get it back.

This is why I stay consistent.

This is why I protect my mornings.

This is why I keep my circle small.

Because my rhythm is my weapon.

And I'm not letting anyone throw it off.

You want to know how to stay locked in?

Don't break your flow.

Build it.

Respect it.

Repeat it.

The rhythm you're in right now?

That's the difference between who you used to be and who you're becoming.

So guard it like your life depends on it.

Because in some ways—it does.

Don't lose your rhythm.
That's where your power lives.

Chapter 46: When No One's Watching

Anyone can perform when the lights are on.

Anyone can post a workout, a study session, a win.

But what are you doing when their's no audience?

When their's no applause?
No likes?
No one checking in?

That's the real you.

That's where the foundation gets built.

In silence.
In the unseen.
In the hours no one talks about.

Discipline isn't proven in public.
It's developed in private.

I've had nights where I was exhausted, but I still hit the work.

Not because someone was watching.

But because I was.

I've had mornings where I didn't feel like moving—but I moved anyway.

Because I made a commitment to myself.

And my standards don't disappear just because the room is empty.

The world might not see your effort.

But you do.

You see the shortcuts.

You feel the skipped reps.

You know when you gave 70% instead of 100.

You carry the weight of your own inconsistency.

And that's why private discipline is everything.

You want to grow?

Move the same in the dark that you do in the light.

Train with the same intensity whether someone's filming or not.

Study like the exam is tomorrow—even when it's months away.

Keep promises to yourself—especially when no one's there to hold you to it.

Because your future isn't built on what people see.

It's built on what they don't.

When no one's watching,
 you build the version of you they'll never be ready for.

Chapter 47: Progress Over Perfection

Perfection is a trap.

It's the lie that says
 "If it's not perfect, it's not worth it."

That mindset keeps people stuck.

Waiting. Hesitating. Overthinking.

But here's the truth:

You don't need perfect.

You need progress.

You don't need a flawless routine.

You need reps.

You don't need perfect motivation.

You need movement.

You don't need every piece figured out.

You just need to do the next right thing—right now.

Some days you'll crush it.

Some days you'll just show up.

Both count.

Because momentum is built in the messy.

I had to let go of perfection—because it was killing my consistency.

If the gym session wasn't perfect—I used to feel like I failed.

If I missed one task, I'd beat myself up.

But that mindset?

It's not sustainable.

What's sustainable?

Stacking effort.

Day by day.

Brick by brick.

You don't fail when things go off track.

You fail when you quit.

So if the day wasn't perfect, cool.

Was it honest?

Was it intentional?

Did you still move?

Then you're good.

Keep going.

Progress over perfection.

Always.

Because perfection isn't real.

But growth? That's earned.

Chapter 48: Stop Waiting

People waste years waiting.

Waiting to feel ready.
Waiting for motivation.
Waiting for the "perfect" time.
Waiting until they're not scared.
Waiting until life slows down.

And that waiting?

It becomes permanent.

The truth is, their is no perfect moment.

There's just now.

And what you choose to do with it.

I used to wait too.

Waited to apply.
Waited to change my routine.
Waited to speak up.
Waited to start over.

And while I waited?

Nothing changed.

Because waiting is just a more comfortable form of quitting.

It feels safe.
It sounds smart.
But it's just another excuse in disguise.

You don't need more time.

You need more urgency.

You don't need more planning.

You need more execution.

You don't need permission.

You need to move.

The best decision I made?

Starting before I was ready.

Showing up before I had it all figured out.

Failing forward—until the reps started hitting.

Whatever you've been putting off?

Do it now.

The new habit.

The clean break.

The early morning.

The next step.

Whatever it is—start.

Because the life you want?

It's not waiting on more time.

It's waiting on you.

Stop waiting.

Start building.

Chapter 49: Start Over as Many Times as You Need

Nobody gets it right the first time.

Not every plan works.

Not every day hits.

Not every season is smooth.

And that's okay.

Because this path?

It's not about getting it perfect.

It's about staying willing to start again.

I've had days where I fell off.
Skipped the work.
Let distractions in.
Lost focus.
Slipped back into old habits.

But I didn't let that become who I am.

I just reset.

And got back to it.

You don't lose because you fall.
You lose when you refuse to evolve.

That doesn't happen through perfection.

It happens through pressure.

Through slip-ups.

Through the days where you didn't feel like it—but came back stronger the next day.

You want to win long-term?

You better learn to start over without shame.

No self-pity.

No guilt.

Just awareness—and adjustment.

So if you're off track?

Start again.

If you stopped showing up?

Start again.

If you feel behind?

Start again.

Starting over isn't weakness.

It's wisdom.

It means you're still in the fight.

Still committed.

Still ready to keep going.

You can restart the day.
 The week.
 The month.
 Your entire life—if that's what it takes.

What matters is that you don't quit.

Start over as many times as you need.
 Just don't stop.

Chapter 50: Respect the Process

Everyone wants the result.

Few want the process.

Because the process is long.
 Quiet.
 Frustrating.
 Exhausting.
 Unseen.

But that's where everything gets built.

Not in the outcome.

In the grind.

The discipline.
The setbacks.
The late nights.
The small wins that no one celebrates.
The days where it doesn't look like it's working—but you show up anyway.

That's the real work.

You don't plant a seed and dig it up tomorrow to see if it's growing.

You water it.
You trust the roots.
You give it time.

Same thing with your goals.

If you quit just because it's slow—you never gave it a real shot.

Because the process doesn't care about your timeline.

It cares about your consistency.

I've learned to stop rushing.

To stop comparing.

To stop panicking just because results aren't immediate.

I respect the process now.

Because I know it's working—even when it's quiet.

Let everybody else chase fast success.

I'm chasing real transformation.

And that takes time.

So if you're in it right now—keep showing up.

Even when it's boring.

Even when it's thankless.

Even when you feel like it's not moving.

Because it is.

Respect the process.
It's making you stronger than you realize.

Chapter 51: Some People Liked You Better When You were Struggling

Let's be real.

Not everyone is going to support your growth.

Some people liked you better when you were distracted.

When you weren't focused.
 When you played small.
 When you didn't believe in yourself.

Why?

Because your discipline exposes their laziness.

Your consistency reminds them of what they're not doing.

Your growth challenges their comfort.

And most people don't want to be challenged.

They want company in their comfort zone.

So when you start rising?

They fall off.

Or worse—they start talking.

"You think you're better than us now?"
"You've changed."
"You used to be fun."
"You're too serious."

Yeah, I changed.

Because staying the same would've killed everything I'm trying to build.

So I stopped trying to convince people.

Stopped trying to bring everyone with me.

Stopped asking for understanding from people who benefited from my weakness.

I got tired of being liked by people who had no intention of growing.

So I grew anyway.

If your glow makes them uncomfortable, that's on them.

If your focus makes them feel left out, that's on them.

If your growth offends their comfort?

Too bad.

You weren't built to stay small so other people could feel tall.

You weren't built to shrink around fragile egos.

You were built to lead by example—even if that means walking alone.

So yeah—some people liked you better weak.

But that version of you?
They don't live here anymore.

Chapter 52: You Are Who You Used to Need

Think back.

Think about the version of you that was lost.

The one who didn't believe in himself—or herself.

The one who was scared, quiet, unsure, just trying to get by.

You remember that version?

Good.

Now look at who you're becoming.

Every rep you hit.

Every early morning you show up for.

Every hard decision you make.

Every distraction you cut off.

You're not just building yourself—you're becoming exactly who that younger version of you needed.

I used to look at people who were locked in and think:

"Damn. I wish I could be like that."

Now I'm that guy.

Because I didn't stop when it got hard.

I didn't waver when everything went still.

I didn't let other people's opinions steer my direction.

You want to know if it's working?

Look at how far you've come.

Not just physically.
 Mentally.

Emotionally.

Spiritually.

You're not who you used to be.

You're someone your younger self would be proud of.

And if you're still becoming that person?

Good.

Don't stop.

Because one day, someone's going to look at you and say:

"If he did it, maybe I can too."

You won't even know you inspired them.

You'll just be living different.

Moving different.

Walking with discipline and fire.

And that will speak louder than any words.

You are who you used to need.
So keep becoming that person.

Chapter 53: You Don't Need a Round of Applause

Most people move for attention.

They only work when someone's watching.
Only post when they think it'll get likes.
Only show discipline when their's an audience.

But you?

You move different.

Because you finally realized—

You don't need a round of applause to validate your work.

You need peace.
You need progress.
You need to keep your promises to yourself.

That's the reward.

I've done some of my best work in silence.

No posts.
No cameras.
No congratulations.

Just me, locked in, doing what needed to be done.

And it felt real.

Because I wasn't doing it to be seen.

I was doing it to grow.

That's the level I operate on now.

Some people need the crowd.

They need feedback just to keep going.

I don't.

Because I'm not performing—I'm becoming.

So don't get confused when nobody claps for you.

It doesn't mean you're not doing something great.

It just means you're not doing it for show.

Keep writing when no one's reading.
Keep training when no one's cheering.
Keep studying when no one's checking.
Keep growing when no one's noticing.

Your results will speak for you.

Louder than applause ever could.

You don't need the claps.
You need the consistency.

Chapter 54: Discipline Feels Better Than Regret

There's two types of pain:

The pain of discipline—
And the pain of regret.

You choose one every day.

Discipline hurts in the moment.
Waking up early.
Staying in when your friends go out.
Training when you're sore.
Studying when you're tired.

But regret?

Regret sticks with you.

It whispers in your head.
It eats at you.

It reminds you what you could've been—if you had just stayed locked in.

I've felt both.

And I'll take the pain of discipline every time.

Because when I finish what I said I would?

When I go to bed knowing I gave it everything?

That peace hits different.

I used to choose comfort over commitment.

And all it got me was delay.
 Frustration.
 Missed opportunities.

Now I move different.

I'd rather sweat today than hate myself tomorrow.

I'd rather suffer through the reps than carry the weight of wishing I had.

Because discipline pays off every time.

Not always in money.
 Not always in praise.

But in peace.

That internal peace that tells you:
"You said you'd do it. And you did."

Regret doesn't offer that.

It offers what-ifs.
It offers shame.
It offers the pain of knowing you gave up.

So yeah—discipline hurts sometimes.

But regret hurts forever.

Discipline feels better than regret.
Every time.

Chapter 55: Tired Doesn't Mean Stop

Everybody gets tired.

That's normal.

But what you do when you're tired?

That's what sets you apart.

You can be tired and still focused.
 You can be tired and still show up.
 You can be tired and still move with purpose.

Tired doesn't mean you're done.

It just means you're in it.

I've trained tired.
 Worked tired.
 Studied tired.
 Sat in class exhausted but still locked in.

Because the mission doesn't care how I feel—it cares if I finish.

You don't need to feel 100% to give 100%.

That means there's more left in you, even when your body says otherwise.

Sometimes the greatest wins come right after the point where you wanted to quit.

Tired is a sign you're working.
 Tired is a signal that you're not just talking—you're doing.

But tired is not a reason to stop.

I'm not saying destroy yourself.

I'm saying don't confuse fatigue with failure.

Know the difference between needing rest—and looking for a way out.

If you really need to reset, reset.

But if you're just uncomfortable?

Push through.

Because every time you move while tired,
 You're proving to yourself that your emotions don't run your life—your discipline does.

Tired doesn't mean stop.
 It means lean in.

Chapter 56: This Isn't the Hardest Thing You've Been Through

When things get heavy, I remind myself of one thing:

This isn't the hardest thing I've been through.

Not even close.

I've lived through real pressure.
I've moved through war zones, silence, doubt, fear.
I've been broke.
I've been counted out.
I've been in situations where "making it" didn't feel possible.

But I did.

So this?

This stress? This deadline? This workout? This routine?

I've faced worse.

You want to stop giving up when things get hard?

Start keeping score.

Look back at what you've survived.
Look at everything you didn't quit through.
Look at the days you thought would break you—but didn't.

That's your fuel now.

All those memories of pain you overcame?

That's your reminder:
You're not soft.
You're not weak.
You're still standing.

The mind tries to panic when things get hard.

But I shut that down.

Because I've got evidence—real, lived evidence—that I can make it through.

And if I could make it through that?

I can make it through this.

That mindset right their?

It turns panic into purpose.

It turns stress into power.

It turns pressure into precision.

You don't need external validation.

You need to remember who you are.

You need to remember where you came from.

And you need to remind yourself—this moment will not be the one that breaks you.

This isn't the hardest thing you've been through.
And it won't be the last.
But you're still built for it.

Chapter 57: When It's Boring, You Keep Going

Everybody shows up when it's exciting.

New plan.
New gym.
New project.
New spark.

That's easy.

But when the routine gets dry?
When the hype dies out?
When it's just repetition and silence?

That's when most people fall off.

But not you.

Because you've learned something they haven't:

The boring part is where the results live.

Progress isn't loud.
It's not flashy.
It's not full of big moments.

It's built in the quiet.
In the reps.
In the grind that feels the same day after day.

That's real.

Because you won't always feel it.

Some days are just clock in, do the work, clock out.

Nothing special.

But it adds up.

I've trained on days when the gym felt like a chore.
I've studied when my brain felt heavy.
I've shown up when everything in me said, "Not today."

And those days?

Those are the ones that built the discipline.

You don't get better because you're excited.

You get better because you're committed.

Anybody can start.

Not everybody can keep going when it's boring.

That's what separates the focused from the fake.

That's what separates the consistent from the casual.

That's what builds you when nothing else will.

So if it feels stale?

Good.

That means you're in the grind zone.

And if you stay in it?

You win.

When it's boring, you keep going.
 That's the difference.

Chapter 58: Lead Yourself First

Everyone wants to lead.

Wants to inspire.
Wants to be respected.
Wants to be followed.

But here's the truth:

You can't lead anyone if you can't lead yourself.

Before you try to motivate others,
before you tell people what they should be doing,
before you start giving advice—check your own habits.

Are you keeping your word to yourself?
Are you moving with discipline when no one's watching?
Are you doing the work, or just talking about it?

I had to ask myself those same questions.

There were times I wanted to lead—but I wasn't even dialed in personally.

Once I fixed that?

Everything changed.

Because real leadership starts when you start fixing your own bad habits

You leads by example.

By consistency.
By pain.
By repetition.

By showing up when it's hard—not when it's easy.

Nobody's coming to check in on your discipline.

Nobody's going to follow up on your early wake-ups.

Nobody's going to force you to grow.

That's on you.

If you want to be respected, lead yourself.

Wake up when you said you would.
Finish what you started.
Keep your circle tight.
Move like someone who sets the standard—not follows it.

The version of you that inspires others?

It's built in silence.

One locked-in decision at a time.

So before you look around to lead others…

Lead yourself first.
And do it without shortcuts.

Chapter 59: Respect Over Attention

It's easy to get attention.

Post something flashy.
Say something wild.
Show off for the camera.
Fake consistency just to look the part.

But respect?

That's earned.

And it's earned in the silence.

People chase likes.
They chase applause.

They chase validation from people who aren't even focused themselves.

But the truth is?

Attention fades.
 Respect lasts.

I've had people ignore me while I was building.

Laugh when I started.

Doubt me when I didn't have the results yet.

Now?

They don't laugh anymore.

Because I never wanted their attention—I wanted to become undeniable.

You don't need claps.

You don't need praise.

You need self-respect.

That internal voice that says,
 "You did what you said you'd do."

Respect is built:

When no one's watching

When the work is boring

When you choose growth over comfort

When you keep showing up while they're distracted

You don't get respected for talking.

You get respected for consistency.

For discipline.
 For clarity.
 For showing up when no one was watching.

Let them chase attention.

You chase impact.

Let them trend.

You train.

Let them play the short game.

You build something that outlasts all of it.

Because when it's all said and done?

Respect is greater than attention.

Every time.

Chapter 60: Do It for you

If you're grinding just to prove people wrong,
 you'll burn out.

If you're chasing goals to make someone jealous,
 you'll lose steam.

If your only motivation is external,
 it won't last.

Because validation fades.
 Attention fades.
 And most of the people you're trying to impress?
 They're not even paying attention.

I had to learn that the hard way.

Early on, I wanted to show people what I could do.
 Make them regret doubting me.
 Make them wish they supported me.

But that kind of fire?

It doesn't burn long.

Now I grind because:

I love who I'm becoming

I respect the work

I refuse to waste what I've survived

I'm building something real that doesn't depend on opinions.

When you do it for you,
  you move different.

You stay consistent when no one's watching.
  You keep showing up when nobody claps.
  You stop performing—and start becoming.

So yeah, let them doubt you.
  Let them talk.
  Let them watch from the sidelines.

Just don't let that be your fuel.

Do it because you know you were built for more.
  Do it because the old version of you is gone.
  Do it because your future deserves everything you've got.

Do it for you.

No one else.

Chapter 61: Motivation Is Optional—Discipline Is Not

Motivation is cool when it shows up.

It feels good.

It gives you a spark.

But it's unreliable.

It comes and goes like the weather.

If you only work when you're motivated,
you're not consistent.

You're just emotional.

I had to kill that mindset.

I used to wait for the "right mood" to hit.

But the longer I waited,
the further I fell behind.

So, I stopped waiting.

Now I move off discipline, not dopamine.

Because motivation won't wake you up at 5AM.
 Motivation won't carry you through injury.
 Motivation won't hold the line when you're tired, bored, or doubting yourself.

Discipline will.

Discipline shows up tired.
 Discipline shows up when the feelings aren't their.
 Discipline gets it done—regardless.

So, if you're struggling right now,
 Stop asking yourself if you're motivated.

Ask if you're committed.

Ask if you're locked in.

Ask if you're still willing to show up when it's inconvenient.

Because that's where the wins are.

In the days you didn't feel it but still showed up.
 In the sets you finished even when your mind wanted to

quit.

In the decisions you made without hype—just standard.

Motivation is a bonus.

Discipline is the requirement.

So yeah—motivation is optional.
Discipline is not.

Chapter 62: Growth Feels Like Discomfort

Everybody wants to grow…
Until it stops feeling good.
Until no one's watching.
Until it gets repetitive.
Until it gets lonely.

But that's what growth is supposed to feel like.

It's not always inspirational.
It's not always clean.
It's not always flashy or Instagram-worthy.

Most of the time?

It feels like pressure.

It feels like:

Waking up earlier than you want to

Saying no when you used to say yes

Training while your body's sore

Studying while your mind is tired

Leaving behind comfort, people, and habits that once made you feel safe

That's it.

Growth is not supposed to feel good.

It's supposed to change you.

And change doesn't happen inside your comfort zone.

Change happens in discomfort.

In resistance.

In pressure.

I felt all three when I started going over radiographic physics—even though I hadn't even started the class yet. I like being ahead of the game. So I dove in. I tried teaching myself all the formulas and math problems that didn't make sense. And yeah—it got frustrating. Nothing clicked.

I watched every video I could find, trying to understand how they got their answers. In my mind I kept thinking, if it makes sense to them, there's a way it can make sense to me.

Quitting? Not an option. I want this too badly. I thought about those physics' problems nonstop. I close my eyes and still see the equations. I kept pushing—despite the distractions. Friends called me to hang out on the weekends. I said no.

I don't need fun.
I'm in my era of growth.

There's no room for distractions. Only growth.

If you're weak in a subject, stay devoted. Stay focused. I promise—if you don't quit, it will eventually make sense. The more I stuck with it, the more things started clicking.

That's where the mindset sharpens.
That's where the body gets tested.
That's where you stop being who you were—and become who you're meant to be.

You want to grow?
You've got to stop chasing the easy route.
You've got to stop waiting for it to "feel right."

You've got to learn to stay calm in chaos.

Grounded in discomfort.

Unshakable when everything around you want you soft.

You don't have to like discomfort.

But you do have to respect it.

Because it's making you better—even if you can't see it yet.

Growth feels like discomfort.

And that's how you know it's working.

Chapter 63: Grateful, but not done

I've come a long way.

I remember when I prayed for the things I have now.

A roof.

Peace.

Direction.

Clarity.

Discipline.

And I'm thankful—every day.

But let's get something straight:

I'm not done.

Being grateful doesn't mean you stop grinding.
It doesn't mean you sit back and get soft.
It doesn't mean you let hunger die just because things got better.

That mindset doesn't stop at milestones.
It keeps building.

I'm proud of how far I've come.
But I still see what's possible.
I still see areas where I can sharpen.
I still know there's more in me.

That's not greed.
That's discipline.

Some people get a little success and start coasting.
They start telling stories instead of writing new ones.

Not me.

I'll celebrate the win—then wake up and look for the next mountain.

Because I didn't survive everything, I've been through just to get comfortable.

I'm not chasing more out of lack.
I'm chasing more because I was built for it.

So yeah—I'm grateful.

But don't confuse that with being finished.

I'm just getting started.

Grateful, but not done.
That's the standard.

Chapter 64: Ready Is a Lie

You'll never feel fully ready.

Not to change your life.
Not to leave comfort behind.
Not to chase something real.
Not to take the risk.
Not to raise your standard.

That feeling you're waiting for?

It's a trap.

I used to think I had to feel confident before I acted.

I thought I needed a perfect plan.
More time.
More clarity.
More approval.

But none of that ever came.

You don't get ready first.

You get ready by moving.

I've taken big steps without a backup plan.

I've gone into rooms where I felt out of place.
Started projects I didn't fully understand.
Committed before I had all the answers.

And guess what?

That's when everything shifted.

If you wait to be ready, you'll wait forever.

Because the mind will always come up with a reason to pause.

But discipline ignores that.

Discipline moves anyway.

You don't need perfect conditions.
You don't need certainty.
You don't need everyone's support.

You need movement.
You need reps.
You need trust—in yourself, in the grind, in the process.

The only way to become ready?

Start.

You're not behind.

You're just one decision away from momentum.

Ready is a lie.
Start anyway.

Chapter 65: Stay Even

Highs will come.

So will lows.

That's life.

That's progress.

But the ones who win?

They don't ride the wave.

They stay even.

They don't get cocky when things go right.

They don't panic when things fall apart.

They keep showing up.

Same pace.

Same standard.

Same pressure—regardless of circumstances.

It's easy to get hyped off a win.

One good workout.

One good week.

One little breakthrough.

But the real question is:

Can you keep your discipline after the celebration fades?

On the flip side—anyone can be focused when things are smooth.

But can you stay consistent when nothing's clicking?

Can you still move forward when life starts pushing back?

That's what "stay even" means.

No extremes.

No drama.

No emotional reactions.

Just pressure. Just motion. Just reps.

Because staying balanced = staying dangerous.

I've seen people get high off their own success—then fall off.

I've seen people break after one loss—because they never learned to hold the line.

Me?

I stay even.

Focused when it's good.

Focused when it's hard.

No switch-up.

No let-up.

Just locked.

Stay even.

That's how you stay in the game.

Chapter 66: Your Name Is a Brand

You don't need a logo.
You don't need a business.
You don't need followers.

You already have a brand.

It's your name.

And every decision you make is either building it—or breaking it.

When you say you'll do something,
and you don't?

That's your brand.

When you show up late,
when you don't show up at all,
when you give half-effort—that's your brand.

No flash.

Nothing extra.

Just reps.

Just real.

That's the power of a name.

Your name follows you when you leave the room.

Your name is mentioned in conversations you're not even part of.

Your name either opens doors—or shuts them.

I started paying attention to what my name meant to people.

Was I known for being locked in?

Or just being reckless?

Was I reliable?

Or unpredictable?

I made a choice:

Let my name represent pressure.

Let it represent follow-through.

Let it represent discipline.

You don't need to explain who you are—your name should speak for itself.

So, ask yourself:

When people hear your name, what do they expect?

When your name is mentioned, what follows?

What habits are shaping the definition of your name?

This is your brand.

Build it with intention.
 Protect it with discipline.

Because it's not just about reputation.

It's about identity.

Your name is a brand.
 Carry it like it matters.

Chapter 67: Character Is the Real Currency

In a world where everybody's trying to flex...

Character is what actually holds weight.

Not your car.

Not your clothes.

Not your followers.

Not your talk.

Who you are when nobody's looking—that's what counts.

You can fake hustle.

You can fake discipline for the camera.

You can post quotes all day.

But when it's just you and the silence?

What's real shows up.

Because when you're alone, and no one's clapping?

You find out who you are.

I've seen people with big voices but small follow-through.

I've seen people talk about growth—but never show it.

I've seen people preach discipline—but give up under pressure.

Why?

Because character wasn't built.

Just the image was.

Your character is your foundation.

And if that cracks, everything on top of it collapses.

I've made decisions no one will ever know about—and I'm proud of those more than the ones that got recognition.

Because doing it right in silence?
That's real.

You want to build something that lasts?

Don't just build hype.

Build honor.
Build consistency.
Build honesty.
Build humility.

Even when it's hard.
Especially when it's hard.

Character is what keeps you strong when the crowd disappears.
Character is what earns real trust.
Character is what makes you unstoppable—because you don't have to pretend.

Character is the real currency.

Spend it wisely.

Chapter 68: Yes—It's Worth It

You ever sit back and think...

"Is all this even worth it?"

The early mornings.

The training.

The silence.

The people who left.

The sacrifices nobody sees.

Yeah—it's worth it.

It's worth it because you're not who you used to be.

It's worth it because now you move different.

You think sharper.

You carry peace.

You lead yourself.

And nobody can put a price on that.

You're not building image.

You're building freedom.

Freedom from doubt.
 Freedom from distractions.
 Freedom from needing approval.
 Freedom from being soft.

That's what this work is for.

That's what makes it worth it.

The internal wins.
 The quiet confidence.
 The discipline that nobody can take from you.

I've lost sleep for this.
 Lost comfort.
 Lost people.

But I gained self-respect.

And that's a trade I'd make every time.

So, when it's hard?
 When you're drained?
 When are you tired of being the one who always shows up?

Just remember:

You're not doing this for applause.

You're doing it because you refused to be average.

Because of the life you want?
The mind you want?
The legacy you want?

It doesn't come easy.
It comes earned.

So yeah—it's worth it.

Even on the hard days.
Especially on the hard days.

Keep going.
It's worth it.

Chapter 69: Potential Means Nothing Without Standards

People love telling you,

"You've got so much potential."

But you know what potential is?

A compliment with no weight—unless you live up to it.

You can have all the talent in the world.
All the skill.
All the tools.

But if you don't show up daily with intention and pressure?

It means nothing.

Potential doesn't get results.
Standards do.

That's the difference.

Potential says,

"You might be great."

Standards say,

"I don't miss. I don't give up. I don't need hype—I execute."

You want to become elite?

Stop fantasizing about what you're capable of,
and start showing what you're made of—on command.

271

This means:

You show up when it's inconvenient

You do the work when no one checks in

You keep your word to yourself—no exceptions

You don't let emotions lower your expectations

Potential talks big at the start.

Standards are quiet—but they last.

I stopped chasing potential a long time ago.

Now I just honor the standard.

And that's what keeps me locked in.

Potential fades.
Standards endure.
Pick the one that builds legacy.

Chapter 70: Master One Thing

Everybody wants to do everything.

Try every hustle.

Touch every lane.

Stack up hobbies.

Stack up side projects.

But here's the truth:

Most people are average at everything because they never committed to mastering anything.

Mastery isn't flashy.

It's not quick.

It's not trending.

What separates the real ones from the busy ones is mental toughness.

Start strong.

Get bored.

Move on.

That was my pattern—until I realized I wasn't building anything. I was just staying distracted.

Now?

I pick something and bleed into it.

I study it.

I show up for it.

I stay when it gets boring.

I hold the line when it gets tough.

Because mastery is about depth, not variety.

It's about focus, not looking around.

The goal is to get so good at one thing,
that they can't ignore you.

To be so disciplined in one lane they have to respect it.

Let everyone else chase trends.

You chase skill.

You chase precision.

You chase dominance in your lane.

Master one thing.

Then move.

But don't leave a place until you've made your mark.

Master one thing.

That's how you become undeniable.

Chapter 71: Finish the Job

Anyone can start.
Few finish.

Starting feels good.
It's new.
It's exciting.
It makes you feel like you're moving.

But starting doesn't build legacy.

Finishing does.

Finishing is different.
Finishing takes grind.
Finishing takes boredom.
Finishing takes pressure.
Finishing means you show up even when you're over it.

I've started things I didn't finish—and I remember the weight of that.

It stays in your head.
It builds doubt.
It eats away at your confidence.

But the first time I finished something hard?

Everything changed.

That mindset stuck with me.

Now I don't care how I feel.
I care if the mission is complete.

I care if I said I would.
I care if I signed up for it.
I care if the standard was met.

Because real confidence comes from one place:

Follow-through.

Let's talk about the people who never follow through.

You've heard it before:

"I almost joined the military."

"I took the ASVAB, but something came up."

"I had personal stuff going on, so I didn't go"

"But if I did join, I would've gone Marine Corps, or Special Ops, or Navy SEAL."

And every time I hear that, I feel the same thing—
disappointment.

Not because they didn't do it.

But because they had the potential.

They had what it takes.

But they didn't want to tap into it.

They didn't want to find out where their real limits were.

They gave up before it even started.

They got scared when it got serious.

People love the identity.

They love how it sounds.

But when it's time to suffer, to commit, to finish?

They vanish.

That's the difference.

If you commit, you follow through.

You don't make excuses.

You don't look back.

You finish the job.

You've got chapters ahead of.

New levels you haven't even seen yet.

But you only get to them by finishing this one.

So when you feel like stopping?

Remember why you started

Remember who's watching

Remember the version of you that's counting on this being finished

Don't leave it halfway.

Don't build a resume of "almost."

Finish the job.
Then rest.
Not the other way around.

Chapter 72: Stop Asking for Permission

You don't need permission to be great.
You don't need permission to start.
You don't need approval to change your life.

You just need to move.

Most people are stuck because they're waiting:

For someone to notice them

For someone to believe in them

For someone to say "Now is the right time"

That waiting turns into years.
 Into frustration.
 Into regret.

I stopped waiting when I realized something:

No one's coming to validate the vision.

It's yours.
 You've got to carry it.
 You've got to build it.
 You've got to protect it—before anyone else sees it.

The moment you stop asking for permission, you move differently.

You stop shrinking to make others comfortable.
 You stop hesitating when you know what needs to be done.

You stop explaining yourself to people who aren't even built for what you're building.

You don't need permission to:

Wake up earlier

Train harder

Speak less

Move smarter

Walk away

Start over

Rise

You just need to decide.

Forget who doesn't understand.
Forget who doubts it.
Forget who left.

This path?
It's yours.

Stop asking for permission.

Start demanding results—from yourself.

Chapter 73: You're Either Making Excuses or Making Progress

You can't do both.

You can't talk about how bad you want it

and still give yourself a way out every time it gets

uncomfortable.

Excuses sound smart.

They sound logical.

They sound like self-care.

But they're slow poison.

They rot your potential while keeping you "comfortable."

At day's end, results matter more than reasons.

I've had excuses before:

"I didn't sleep enough."

"I'll start fresh Monday."

"One missed session doesn't matter."

"At least I showed up yesterday."

None of those took me anywhere.

Every time you make an excuse,

you trade away your momentum.

You delay your breakthrough.

You signal to yourself that the standard doesn't matter.

And once you do that?

Everything else gets easier to walk away from.

In the Marine Corps, they have an acronym for everything.

It makes things easier to memorize, even when they seem

impossible at first.

No matter how hard it is to remember all those acronyms, the

Drill Instructors drill them into you — over and over — until

you start repeating things you never thought you'd remember.

That taught me something: anything is possible — whether

it's passing a class, earning a certification, or chasing a goal

that feels out of reach.

If you set aside the time, stay consistent, and stop looking for

a way out, you can do it.

It just takes initiative — the decision to stop making excuses

and start moving.

Your future self will thank you for taking that leap of faith.

You want to build self-respect?

Cut the excuses.

I learned to replace "I can't" with "Watch me."

Replace every "maybe tomorrow" with "Now."

It doesn't have to be perfect.

It just has to be done.

Today.

Not later.

Not when it's easier.

Not when it's pretty.

Now.

Because every excuse you drop

creates space for progress to grow.

You're either making excuses

or making progress.

Pick one.

Then move.

Chapter 74: Pick one—comfort or growth

You can't have both.

Comfort will give you ease,
 but it won't give you progress.

Growth will give you pressure,
 but it builds everything you say you want.

One will keep you still.
 The other will change your life.

Comfort feels good in the moment.
 But it keeps your mind soft.
 Your body lazy.
 Your standards low.

Growth doesn't always feel good.
 But it will sharpen your discipline.
 Force your focus.
 Test your patience.

And it will build you.

Every day, you pick one:

You hit snooze or you get up.

You scroll or you study.

You talk about it or you train for it.

I had to stop chasing what felt easy.
I had to stop lowering the standard just because it was a long day.

Now?

I pick growth.

Even when it sucks.
Even when I don't feel like it.

Because I know the reward isn't in relief.

It's in the reps.

You want to be uncommon?

You want to live at a different level?

Start with this question:

Am I picking comfort... or growth?

You only get to choose one.

Pick growth.
And don't look back.

Chapter 75: Stay Hungry Even After You Win

The worst thing you can do after a win?

Get comfortable.

That's when most people fall off.

They hit a goal and start coasting.
They ease up.
They celebrate too long.
They start letting things slide.

And just like that?

They lose the edge.

Wins aren't permission to relax.
They're a warning to lock in even harder.

Because the minute you start feeling "arrived,"
You stop evolving.

Why?

Because the real ones don't chase trophies.
They chase pressure.
They chase the version of themselves that's still in the fight.

I've had little wins.

Moments I could've sat back and coasted.

But every time I did that?

I got soft.

Now I train like I'm behind.

I study like I'm losing.

I prep like I haven't made it—because I haven't.

And that mindset?

Keeps me sharp.

Celebrate your win.

Then show up the next day even hungrier.

Because that's what keeps you dangerous.

Let the average get lazy.

Let them start slipping.

Let them pat themselves on the back for doing the minimum.

You?

Stay in the fire.

I'm speaking to those who refuse to settle.

You've got to realize that a diamond is forged under extreme heat and pressure.

Nothing strong comes from living soft.

Live under constant pressure.

Stay in the fire.

And let that version of you shine like a diamond.

I promise—because that's where your true potential starts.

I've had little wins.

Moments I could've sat back and coasted.

But every time I did that, I got soft.

Now I train like I'm behind,

I study like I'm losing.

I prep like I haven't made it—because I haven't.

And that mindset?

Keeps me sharp.

Stay hungry—even after you win.

That's how you stay ready.

Chapter 76: Just Show Up

Some days you'll feel locked in.

Other days you won't.

That's life.

But success doesn't care how you feel.

It only asks one question:

Did you show up or not?

Showing up is the baseline.

Not the bonus.

Not the exception.

The standard.

That means:

You go to the gym when it's raining.

You hit the books when you're tired.

You train when no one's watching.

You clock in when motivation is gone.

And still dominates.

Because discipline doesn't wait for the perfect mood.

Discipline shows up.
 Every time.

You want to shift your identity?

Start with this:

Be the person who shows up.

Not sometimes.

Not when it's easy.

Every day.

Even when it's inconvenient.

Even when it's quiet.

Even when you don't feel like it.

Especially then.

The more you show up,

the less your excuses control you.

The more your confidence grows.

The stronger your mindset becomes.

Forget perfection.

Forget the hype.

Just show up.

And do the work.

Chapter 77: It's Not Supposed to Be Easy

Stop waiting for the struggle to end.

Stop hoping it gets lighter.
Stop wishing it would just flow.

Because once you understand this?

Everything changes:

It's not supposed to be easy.

Growth is hard.
Discipline is uncomfortable.
Change is heavy.

But that's exactly why it works.

If it was easy,
everyone would do it.
Everyone would be locked in.
Everyone would be built different.

But they're not.

Because they chase ease.

You?

You chase strength.

I've had days where everything felt heavy.
And I still showed up.

Not because I'm special.

But because I stopped expecting it to feel good.

When you accept that it's supposed to hurt sometimes,
that's when you stop flinching.
That's when you stop breaking.
That's when you build real grit.

The people looking for shortcuts?

They never last.

The ones who embrace the weight?

They come out unshakable.

So next time it gets hard?

Don't complain.
Don't retreat.
Don't get surprised.

Look it in the face—and keep going.

Because this life?
This discipline?
This mission?

It's not supposed to be easy.
It's supposed to make you stronger.

Chapter 78: This Is Just the Beginning

Seventy-eight chapters deep.
But this isn't the finish line.

It's proof.

Proof that discipline stacks.

That silence works.

That staying locked in pays off.

Most people don't make it this far.

They start strong.

Then fade out.

They talk big.

But break early.

You?

You stayed in the fight.

And that's the truth — for me too.

I stopped making excuses.

Even now, I'm seventy-eight chapters in, and while I'm working, I'm writing down my next ideas — what I'll talk about next, how I'll push the message further.

When I stopped making excuses, I started seeing results in everything.

My schooling?

I passed anatomy I with labs, anatomy II with labs, physics with labs, and chemistry with labs.

I remember my advisor looking at my schedule and saying, "That's a bit aggressive."

She asked, "What if you fail those classes?"

She told me to take it easy.

But I already deleted the words "easy" and "excuses" from my dictionary.

I'm in grind mode.

I'm so hungry I can't sleep at night.

I literally dream about my book, my school assignments, and the next mission I'm going to take on.

This book isn't about hype.

It's about standards.

It's about showing up.

It's about grinding past the excuses.

And that's the truth.

You're not writing a conclusion.

You're building a life.

A mindset.

A name.

A standard that doesn't depend on mood, motivation, or applause.

This chapter isn't about celebration.

It's about confirmation.

You're built different.

And the proof is in the pages.

In the reps.

In the way you didn't quit when it got repetitive.

Now you move with proof.

Now your name carries weight.

Now you walk with receipts.

But don't slow down.

Don't get soft just because people clap.

Stay quiet.

Stay dangerous.

Stay locked.

Because even after seventy-eight chapters in?

This is just the beginning.

Chapter 79: This Is Just How I Move Now

I don't wake up and ask myself if I feel like it.

I don't wait for a spark.

I don't check if I'm in the mood.

I don't need hype.

I don't need a reason.

This is just how I move now.

Discipline isn't a choice anymore.

It's who I am.
It's baked into my routine.
It's locked into my mindset.

Because it's not optional.
It's standard.

And that's where I am now.

I don't need to explain it.
I don't need validation.
I don't need people to understand.
The lifestyle is speaking.
The silence says everything.

You want to know what consistency looks like?

It's not exciting.

It's repetitive.
It's clean.
It's quiet.
It's daily.

I'm not here for moments.

I'm here for momentum.

This isn't a "grind phase."
This isn't a temporary.

This is permanent.
This is embedded.
This is my identity now.

I eat different.
I think different.
I move different.

And it's not up for discussion.

This is just how I move now.

And I'm not going back.

Chapter 80: Growth Will Cost You Some People

When you start getting serious.

When you raise your standard.

When you stop doing what everybody else is doing.

People will fall off.

And that's part of it.

It's not beef.

It's not drama.

It's just alignment.

You're not on the same frequency anymore.

The old version of you needed them.

The new version of you?

Doesn't.

"If you're not willing to sacrifice who you are for who you
will become, you'll never be who you want to be."

And sometimes that sacrifice?

Is people.

People who:

Want to keep you distracted

Want to joke about things you take serious

Call your discipline "too much"

Disappear when the work starts

Only hit you up when they want to pull you backward

I don't hate them.

I just don't move with them anymore.

Because I'm not shrinking to fit the past.

I'm expanding into my future.

Some people only liked you when you weren't locked in.

When you were available for every invite.

When you didn't have goals.

When you were just "cool" with staying average.

Now you're quiet.

Now you're disciplined.

Now you're hard to reach.

That's growth.

You're not leaving people behind to flex.

You're leaving them behind because you refuse to lower your standard to keep their comfort.

Let them say you changed.

You did.

And you're not going back.

Growth will cost you some people.
Pay it.
And keep moving.

Chapter 81: Discipline Brings Clarity

Most people think discipline is about doing more.

Waking up earlier.
Working harder.
Saying no to distractions.

But the truth is—discipline gives you clarity.

When you lock in,
you start seeing things for what they are.

You stop wasting time on things that don't build you.

You stop giving energy to people who drain you.

You stop saying "yes" just to be nice.

Discipline simplifies everything.

You don't overthink.

You don't overcommit.

You don't chase fake validation.

You just move with purpose—every day.

That's what happens when your life is built on real structure—not just emotion.

I used to be scattered.

Too many tabs open.

Saying "yes" to things that didn't align.

Letting other people set my pace.

Not anymore.

Now I move off discipline—and everything around me is cleaner.

Fewer fake friends.
Fewer wasted hours.
Fewer regrets.

More focus.
More progress.
More peace.

If you feel stuck, lost, or overwhelmed—don't go looking for answers in distractions.

Lock in your habits.

Your structure will clear your vision.

Discipline brings clarity.
And clarity builds freedom.

Chapter 82: Hold the Standard When No One's Checking

It's easy to go hard when eyes are on you.

When the team's watching.
When the camera's rolling.
When someone's tracking your moves.

But what about when it's just you?

No one to impress.
No one to correct you.
No one to clap.

That's where it gets real.

Your discipline isn't proven when someone's watching.

It's proven when no one is.

That's elite.

That's where I'm at now.

I don't need a trainer to tell me to push harder.

I don't need a reminder to stay locked in.

I don't need a schedule to move with intent.

The standard is set—and I'm not dropping it for anybody.

If I say I'm going to do something, I do it.

Not because someone will notice.

 But because I notice.

And I refuse to lose respect for myself just to feel comfortable.

This is what separates the locked from the lazy:

Lazy waits to be pushed.

Locked in pushes themselves.

Lazy needs reminders.

Locked in doesn't miss.

Lazy fades in silence.

Locked in levels up when no one's looking.

So if you're in a season where nobody's checking on you?

Good.

That's where your next level gets built.

Hold the standard.
Especially when no one's watching.
That's when it matters most.

Chapter 83: Your Why Is Yours—Protect It

People will ask why you train so hard.
Why you eat a certain way.
Why you don't go out anymore.
Why you're always working.
Why you're always focused.

You don't owe them an answer.

Your why is yours.

Most people won't understand.
Because they're not supposed to.

They didn't feel the pain that shaped you.
They didn't come from what you came from.
They didn't go through what you survived.

So how could they understand your fire?

I stopped explaining my grind.

It's not for approval.
It's not for show.
It's personal.

There's a reason I wake up early.
There's a reason I don't cut corners.
There's a reason I move with this much intensity.

And that reason?

Isn't up for debate.

Protect your why like it's sacred.

Because it is.

It's what keeps you going on the hard days.
It's what keeps you locked when it's quiet.
It's what makes this personal—and permanent.

So the next time someone asks:

"Why do you go so hard?"

Just smile.

And keep moving.

Your why is yours.
Protect it.
Don't explain it.
Let it fuel you.

Chapter 84: They Won't Get It—Do It Anyway

You're going to lose people by being disciplined.

You're going to get judged for being consistent.

You're going to get laughed at for moving serious in a world that plays around.

Let them.

You're not here to be understood.

You're here to be disciplined.

And most people won't get it.

Because they've never taken anything seriously long enough to grow.

You start eating clean, they'll say you're doing too much.

You stay home to work, they'll say you changed.

You train in silence, they'll call you antisocial.

That's fine.

I used to want people to understand why I was grinding.

Why I stopped showing up to every invite.

Why I went quiet.

Why I tightened up my life.

Now?

I don't care if they get it.

Because the ones who get it
 Are probably grinding too.

And the ones who don't?
 Weren't supposed to come with me anyway.

You don't need permission to change.
 You don't need support to stay disciplined.
 You don't need anyone to clap for your process.

You just need to stay with it.

Let them talk.

Let them laugh.

Let them doubt.

You?

Keep showing up.

They won't get it.

Do it anyway.

You're not building for them.

Chapter 85: Save Yourself

No one's coming.

Not your friends.

Not your family.

Not your boss.

Not the system.

It's on you.

And that's not bad news.

That's power.

Because once you accept that no one's going to carry you—
you start carrying yourself.

Fix what's broken.

Build what's missing.

Earn what wasn't given.

There's no rescue squad for people who keep themselves
average.

There's no "right time" coming.

There's no superhero walking through the door.

It's you.

You're the one who has to stop making excuses.

You're the one who has to change your routine.

You're the one who has to break the patterns.

No one's going to want it for you.

And once you stop waiting?

You start building.

You start thinking different.
Moving different.
Carrying yourself like a weapon—not a victim.

You don't need saving.
You need action.
You need structure.
You need belief—and then discipline to back it up.

Every time you show up for yourself,
you prove that you're not weak anymore.
You're not stuck.
You're not lost.

You just needed to decide.

Save yourself.

No one's coming.

And that's the best thing that could've happened to you.

Chapter 86: You Didn't Come This Far to Stop Here

Look at everything you've survived.
Everything you've pushed through.
All the nights you were tired.
All the days you were doubted.

And you're still here.

That means something.

You didn't push through the pain
Just to break when things got calm.

You didn't earn this mindset
Just to coast now that it's steady.

You didn't rebuild yourself
Just to stall out.

You've already paid too much to quit.

Time.
Energy.
Sacrifice.
Isolation.

Why stop now?

Because there were times I thought I had nothing left—
Then kept going for weeks.

That means the tank wasn't empty.

My mindset was.

When it gets hard, remind yourself:
You've been through worse.

You didn't give up then.

You're not giving up now.

You're here for something bigger.

And you haven't even hit your ceiling yet.

You've built discipline.

You've earned clarity.

You've got momentum.

Now multiply it.

This is not the end.

It's the next level.

You didn't come this far to stop here.

You came this far to go even further.

Chapter 87: The Finish Line Is Where Most People Quit

You'd think the closer people get to the goal,
 the harder they'd push.

But that's not what happens.

Most people?
 They slow down.

They see the finish line
 And start coasting.

They let their foot off the gas
 Because they think "close enough" is good enough.

But you?

You're not most people.

You didn't build this fire just to cool off now.

You didn't stack all these pages just to fizzle out in the last few.

You finish strong.

Every time.

I learned that coasting late = regret later.

If I gave 90% the whole way,
  but only gave 50% at the end?

That stain sticks.

And I don't move like that anymore.

When you're close, you go harder.
  You lock in tighter.
  You raise your output—because that last stretch?

That's what people remember.

Anyone can start strong.

Not everyone can finish sharp.

So whatever you're closing in on—
This book, your goals, your mindset, your next level—

Don't let up.

Finish like it matters.

The finish line is where most people quit.
You're not most people.
You finish stronger than you started.

Chapter 88: Stay Sharp

You can be good—
And still go harder.

You can be ahead—
And still train like you're behind.

You can have wins—

And still move like you've got something to prove.

That's how you stay sharp.

The minute you relax,
 you start slipping.

Not because you're weak—
But because your edge gets dull when you stop using it.

I've seen people lose their fire after a little success.
 They start showing up late.
 They stop prepping with intent.
 They stop training with urgency.

Why?

Because they got soft off progress.

Me?

I keep my blade sharp with:

Quiet mornings

Heavy work

Hard reading

Tight routines

High standards

Even when no one's checking.
Even when I don't feel like it.

If you want to stay dangerous?

Stay ready.

Stay disciplined.

Stay uncomfortable.

You don't need to be loud.
You just need to stay sharp.

Stay sharp.

Every day.

No matter how far you've come.

Chapter 89: Act Like You're Still Behind

You're ahead of the old you.

You've done what most people won't.

You've built discipline, consistency, and pressure.

But don't let that trick you.

You're not done.

Act like you're still chasing something.

Because you are.

The second you start acting like you made it,

you stop moving with intent.

The second you think you're too far ahead to lose,
you slow down.

But when you move like you're still behind?

You stay dangerous.

That's the secret of the locked-in:

They could be first in the room—
And still work like they're last.
They could have momentum—
And still show up like underdogs.

Me?

I never let myself believe I've arrived.

Because the moment you think the job's done,
you start giving less.

So I move like I'm behind.

Like someone out their is working harder.

Like I still haven't hit my ceiling.

Because I haven't.

Let other people relax.

Let them celebrate early.

Let them believe their progress means they're safe.

You?

Stay moving like you've got something to prove.

Because that hunger?

That's the reason you're still here.

Act like you're still behind.

That's how you stay ahead.

Chapter 90: You're Built for This

You didn't get here by accident.
You didn't survive by luck.
You didn't stay consistent by chance.

You earned this.

All those early mornings?
All those silent reps?
All those nights you could've quit?

You didn't.

You stayed.

You suffered.
You focused.
You grew.

You're not soft.
You're not fragile.
You're not stuck.

You're built for this.

But not everybody proves it.

You did.

And you're still proving it.

The obstacles?
 You didn't run.

The setbacks?
 You didn't break.

The silence?
 You didn't stop.

That means something.

That means this discipline isn't a phase.
 It's who you are now.

That means the mindset is yours.

And it's only getting stronger.

I've had to remind myself of that, too.

When things feel heavy.

When the grind feels long.

When the results come slow.

I stop and say it straight:

I'm built for this.

I've shown it.

And I'm not done.

You don't need motivation.

You need memory.

Memory of how far you've come.

What you've overcome.

Who you used to be—and who you refuse to be again.

So say it and mean it:

I'm built for this.

I've earned it.

And I'll keep showing it.

Chapter 91: It Was Always You

Every rep.

Every step.

Every quiet decision.

Every early morning and late night...

That was you.

Not luck.

Not someone saving you.

Not someone giving you a handout.

Just you.

You made the decision to keep going.

You made the decision to start over.

You made the decision to grind in silence while everyone else was sleeping or scrolling.

You stopped waiting.
You stopped blaming.
You stopped playing small.

You got quiet.
You got focused.
You got consistent.

And now you're here.

It's easy to forget how far you've come.
Easy to overlook your own progress because you've been too locked in to reflect.

But take a second and own this:

You did this.

You wrote this.
You lived this.
You became this.

And you're still just getting started.

No one built you.

No one forced this discipline.

No one wrote these pages for you.

It was always you.

So, finish strong.

Keep moving.

And never forget:

It was always you.

Chapter 92: Discipline Over Distractions

It's not just laziness that ruins people.

It's distraction.

One minute of scrolling turns into an hour.

One missed assignment turns into dropping a class.

One skipped workout turns into quitting entirely.

It doesn't happen all at once.

It creeps in.

And if you're not locked in, you won't even notice it.

Right now, everybody's distracted.

Notifications, drama, news, trends, opinions—it never ends.

People are tuned in to everything except themselves.

They know what celebrities are doing but can't even tell you what goals they've set for the week.

That's not how I live.

I treat my focus like it's currency.

Because it is.

You only get so much attention each day.

If you spend it on nonsense, don't be surprised when you come up short.

That's why I limit distractions.

I don't need to know what everybody's doing.

I need to know what I'm doing.

Where I'm headed.

What's due this week. What I need to study. What I need to improve.

Everything else is just distraction.

I keep all my notifications off.

Texts. Apps. Social media. I don't see any of it unless I go check it myself.

So, when people say, "Did you see what I sent you?" I'm like—"Nope. Never saw it."

And I'm not lying.

The only notification I allow is from my mom.

When she calls, everything stops.

That's the only alert I answer immediately. Because of what she's done for me, how she raised me, what she sacrificed, I owe her everything.

And even though I could never repay her, I can still respect her like that.

Everything else?

Silenced.

People think I'm ignoring them, but I'm not.

I'm just busy staying locked in.

And if you're a distraction?

I'm sorry—but you'll have to find someone else to distract.

Protecting your focus means being okay with silence.

With discipline.

With being misunderstood.

Some people think you're antisocial because you don't waste time.

They don't get it.

That's fine.

You're not here to be understood.

You're here to get it done.

When I sit down to study, I don't have my phone next to me.

When I train, I'm not filming it for likes.

When I say I'm going to do something—I lock in until it's done.

That's how I move.

There's always going to be something fighting for your attention.

But not everything deserves it.

Ask yourself:

Is this making me better?

Is this building something?

Is this pulling me closer to where I said I want to be?

If the answer is no—cut it.

Time is too expensive to waste.

Even when life gets loud—I stay quiet.

Even when people move wild—I stay steady.

Even when it would be easier to chill—I stay sharp.

Because distractions are temporary.

But so are opportunities.

If you get caught up in the distraction, you'll miss your shot.

Protect your focus.

Like your future depends on it.

Because it does.

Everybody wants to be seen.

Wants to be heard.

Wants to be "known."

That's the trap.

You get addicted to attention, and then you start performing instead of producing.

You start chasing claps instead of stacking wins.

You start living for validation instead of results.

I don't move like that.

I don't tell people what I'm working on.

I just work.

Quietly.

Early mornings. Long nights. No announcements. No status updates.

I'd rather be underestimated and overdeliver.

Because silence is powerful.

It throws people off.

You ever notice the loudest person in the room usually has the least going on?

Always talking. Always selling something. Always trying to prove a point.

I'm the opposite.

I don't need to explain myself.

My effort speaks louder than my mouth ever could.

Moving in silence doesn't mean hiding.

It means you don't need approval to get started.

You don't wait for someone to co-sign your vision.

You don't need permission to rise.

You don't chase hype. You chase progress.

Every goal I've hit—I kept to myself first.

I planned it. Executed it. Finished it.

Then let the results speak when it was already done.

People ask me, "Why don't you post more?"

Because I'm too busy building.

Because if I spend all day documenting my grind, that means
I'm not actually grinding.

I'm not here to perform.

I'm here to be solid.

I don't need likes. I need structure.

I don't need comments. I need commitment.

I don't need claps. I need consistency.

There's something powerful about being the one nobody sees coming.

No warning. No buildup. Just results.

That's how I want to show up in the world.

Let people sleep on you.

Let them think you're not working.

Let them think you've disappeared.

And when it's time, show them everything you did while they were talking.

The more I grow, the less I speak.

Not because I'm shy.

But because I'd rather show you discipline than talk about it.

Because the people who are really locked in?

They don't need to explain themselves.

They're too busy doing the work.

So yeah—I move in silence.

Not because I'm hiding.

But because the best moves don't make noise.

Your energy is your currency.

You spend every day—on people, habits, thoughts, conversations, distractions.

If you don't control where it goes, it will disappear—and take your peace with it.

I learned this the hard way.

Giving too much of myself to people who didn't value it.

Saying yes to stuff that drained me.

Engaging in things that didn't match my vision.

And at the end of the day, I'd wonder why I felt off.

It wasn't weakness.
 It was energy leaks.

Now?

I protect my energy like my future depends on it.

Because it does.

I don't respond to everything.

I don't chase every invite.

I don't argue with people who aren't trying to grow.

I don't explain myself to people committed to misunderstanding me.

That's wasted fuel.

And I need my fuel to build.

People will drain you just by being inconsistent.

Just by being scattered and aimless.

Just by being near your space with the wrong mindset.

If you don't filter it, you'll absorb it.

If your circle doesn't sharpen you?

It's a cage.

If your habits don't elevate you?

They're weights.

If your environment doesn't support your goals?

It's time to leave it behind.

People think discipline is about waking up early and working hard.

It's deeper than that.

It's about saying no.

To fake friends.

To timewasters.

To laziness in disguise.

To anything that doesn't fuel the version of you you're becoming.

You don't have to explain why you're unavailable.

You don't owe anyone access to your energy.

You're allowed to say:

"I'm focused."

"I'm building."

"I'm locked in."

And then move without guilt.

Your energy is sacred.

Protect it with your routine.

Protect it with your boundaries.

Protect it with your habits.

Because once it's gone—you can't get that time back.

Protect your energy like it's the foundation of your future.

Because it is.

People think silence means weakness.

Like if you're quiet, you must not have anything to say.

But silence?

It's one of the strongest things you can master.

I've learned that not every battle needs a response.

Not every comment deserves attention.

Not every insult requires a comeback.

Sometimes the best answer is no answer.

Just focus.

Just discipline.

Just work.

I've had people doubt me out loud.

Try to challenge me.

Try to bait me into drama, arguments, competition I didn't sign up for.

They wanted a reaction.

All they got was silence.

Because I don't argue with people I'm not trying to become.

Silence isn't a weakness.

It's control.

It's strength without noise.

It's moving without needing to announce every step.

You ever notice the loudest in the room usually haven't done the work?

They talk more than they work.

Post more than they progress.

But the ones really putting in the hours?

They're too busy building to explain themselves.

The disciplined ones speak through their results.

they speak when it matters.

Silence is where the mindset gets sharpened.

No distractions. No opinions. Just the truth.

It's where you check yourself.

It's where you get honest with where you're slipping.

And where you tighten everything up.

You don't have to broadcast your moves.

You don't need to prove anything to people who aren't building with you.

Let them guess.

Let them talk.

Let them sleep.

You just keep showing up—quietly dangerous.

If they can't read you, they can't stop you.

347

So, sit with your goals in silence.

Train in silence.

Study in silence.

Let your success make the noise—when it's done.

Not before.

Silence is a skill.

Master it—and you move differently.

Not everything deserves a reaction.

Not every comment needs a clapback.
Not every opinion needs your defense.
Not every challenge deserves your time.

Most of the time?

Silence speaks louder.

When people try to bring you down,
when they question your moves,
when they say, "You've changed,"—

let them.

You don't have to explain growth to people committed to staying the same.

Because once you master your mind?

Other people's opinions lose power.

You want to stay focused?

Learn to stop responding to every distraction that shows up in your inbox, your feed, or your circle.

Silence is discipline.
Silence is self-control.
Silence is strength.

And the people who talk the loudest?

They're usually doing the least.

I don't need to argue about my progress.

I don't need to post every move.

I don't need to prove anything.

I just need to stay consistent.

Let them wonder.

Let them assume.

Let them gossip.

You?

Keep moving.

Because by the time they realize how serious you were?

It'll be too late for them to catch up.

Your focus is too expensive to waste on noise.

So, don't.

Let silence be your response.
 Let results do the talking.

You wouldn't leave your wallet on the street.

You wouldn't let someone walk into your house and take your phone.

So why do you let people steal your energy?

Your time?

Your peace?

I treat my peace like currency now.

Because it pays for my focus.

It keeps me sharp.

It keeps me moving clear, not clouded.

I used to respond to everything.

Every text.
 Every invite.
 Every random drama someone threw my way.

Now?

If it doesn't add value, I don't touch it.

Protecting your peace doesn't mean you're anti-social.

It means you're intentional.

It means you don't give access to people who don't match your effort.

That might mean:

Not answering your phone past a certain time

Saying no to invites that lead to bad habits

Cutting off people who only call when they need something

Spending more time alone with your thoughts, not your notifications

People think they can waste your time just because they're bored.

Let them be bored somewhere else.

Your peace is sacred.

Your routine is sacred.

And if they think you're "acting different" because you're unavailable?

Good.

That means it's working.

I'm not ignoring anyone.

I'm just locked in.

I'm just choosing to protect what I'm building.

I'm just making sure I don't trade purpose for popularity.

Protect your peace like it's money.
 Because without it, you'll spend your life broke—mentally, emotionally, and spiritually.

Chapter 93: Keep Showing Up

There are going to be days when the weight feels too heavy.

When your head's not right.

When you're overwhelmed, under pressure, and ready to break.

And guess what?

You still have to handle it.

Nobody's coming to save you.

No one's going to step in and finish the reps.

No one's going to turn in your assignments, fix your finances, or heal your mind.

That's your job.

I've been there.

Tired. Burned out. Overthinking everything.

And the world just kept spinning.

No pause button.

No relief.

Just me, standing in the middle of it all, knowing the only option was to show up anyway.

It's not about being unbreakable.

It's about being unwilling to quit.

Even when it sucks.

Even when you don't have the answers.

Even when you're carrying more than people know.

You still show up and handle it.

You don't become stronger by avoiding the weight.

You get stronger by carrying it, over and over, until it no longer breaks you.

No more excuses.

No more complaining.

No more waiting for someone to fix it for me.

I woke up. I assess what's in front of me.
And I handle it.

Even if I'm tired.

Even if I'm overwhelmed.

Even if nobody claps.

Because if I drop the ball, everything I've built starts slipping.
And I didn't come this far to let it fall apart now.

You want peace? Handle your responsibilities.
You want strength? Handle your pain.

You want respect? Handle your discipline.
You want a future? Handle your now.

No matter what shows up in your day, in your mind, or in
your life...
Handle it anyway.

Your mind will lie to you.
It'll say,
"You're too tired."
"You've done enough."
"You can skip this one time."

And if you listen?
That one turns into ten.

The real ones?
They don't ask themselves how they feel.
They ask themselves what needs to be done.
And then they do it.

I've had days when my body said no.
When my schedule was packed.
When my brain was foggy, my motivation was zero, and the
last thing I wanted was structure.

But I showed up anyway.

And that made the difference.

Not the hype days.

The hard days.

Because the hard days are where discipline gets forged.

If I say I'm training, I train.

If I say I'm studying, I open the book.

If I say I'm writing, I put words down.

Even when I feel off.

Even when I feel behind.

Even when I feel like disappearing.

Because one day missed becomes two.

And two becomes momentum—in the wrong direction.

I'd rather show up at 50% than wait around for 100%.

Because the truth is?

100% doesn't come often.

You get stronger every time you show up despite the excuses.

You build grit.

You build self-respect.

You teach your mind that you're not ruled by emotion, you're ruled by intention.

So, the next time your mood tries to talk you out of it?

Remember this:

Your mood is temporary.

But your goals are permanent.

Show up anyway.

Success isn't exciting most days.

It's repetitive.

Uncomfortable.

Monotonous.

It's waking up early, doing the same workout, following the same schedule, eating the same meals, studying when no one's watching, writing when no one's clapping.

And doing it again tomorrow.

The results come from boring.

Not hype.

Not motivation.

Just boring, consistent, locked-in reps.

Most people never make it because they get bored.

They crave stimulation.

They want every day to feel like a highlight reel.

But real growth?

It's quiet.

It's tucked away in the days that all look the same.

No glory. Just effort.

No spotlight. Just suffering.

I've had weeks when nothing felt new.

Same gym. Same class. Same routines.

And that's exactly where I grew the most.

Because while everyone else was chasing new?

I was chasing better.

Better form.

Better focus.

Better effort.

Success doesn't come from trying everything.

It comes from mastering something.

Over and over until it becomes part of who you are.

You want to stand out?

Get so good at boring that it becomes natural.

Get so consistent that people ask,

"How do you keep doing this?"

And all you say is,

"I do it because I promised myself I would."

That's it.

That's the mindset.

Fall in love with boring.

Because that's where the real ones are made.

Discipline doesn't care about how you feel.

Success doesn't care if you're in the mood.

Your goals don't ask if you're tired or overwhelmed.

They only respond to execution.

If every decision you make is based on how you feel?

You're never going to be consistent.

Because your feelings change.

Your mood swings.

Your energy goes up and down.

But the mission?

That stays the same.

There were mornings I didn't want to get out of bed.

Nights I didn't want to study.

Days I didn't want to show up.

But I did it anyway.

I refused to negotiate with my own weakness.

And that only happens when you stop letting emotions decide your pace.

I don't wait to feel ready.
I don't wait for ideal conditions.
I move because it's required.

Feelings are temporary.
Standards are permanent.

And once I set a standard?
It doesn't matter if I'm mad, tired, drained, or bored.
I follow through.

Because that's what separates real discipline from fake hype.
Most people wait to "feel like it."
But the truth is, the ones who win?
Do it whether they feel like it or not.

So, stop being emotional about the work.

Do it when it's boring.
Do it when it's lonely.
Do it when nobody claps.
Do it when your energy's low.

Because that's when it counts.

You can feel everything.

Just don't let it stop you.

Do the work.

No matter what.

Progress is quiet.

It doesn't always show up in mirror selfies or report cards.

Sometimes it shows up in how you think.

In what you tolerate.

In how fast you bounce back.

Most people quit because they don't feel like they're making progress.

They want instant change. Visible proof.

But real growth?

It's subtle.

You're further than you think.

If you're waking up earlier than you used to...

If you're saying no to things that used to distract you...

If you're doing the work even when no one's watching...

That's progress.

Sometimes stuck means you're in the grind zone.
The place where nothing feels flashy, but everything's being built.

You're not where you were last year.
Not mentally. Not physically. Not spiritually.
Even if it doesn't feel dramatic, it's real.

That little voice in your head that tells you to show up?
That didn't exist before.

The discipline you carry now?
That didn't happen by accident.
You built that.
Brick by brick.

Progress isn't always loud.
Sometimes it looks like holding your ground when life tries to knock you off it.
Sometimes it looks like not quitting—again.
Sometimes it looks like a small decision with a big ripple.

So, if today feels slow?
If the results aren't showing up fast enough
Just remember this:
You're further than you think.
And the only way you lose now... is if you stop.

You can be talented.

You can be motivated.

You can even have the best intentions.

But if you're not consistent?

None of it matters.

Discipline without consistency fades.

Motivation without consistency dies.

Goals without consistency stay goals.

What changes you?

The reps.

The early mornings.

The boring days.

The small wins.

Stacked over time.

I don't care how fired up you are today.

I care what you do when the hype wears off.

The difference between people who "tried" and people who became?

Consistency.

I don't care if today is exciting.

I care that I show up.

No matter what the mood.

No matter who's watching or not.

You can't cheat consistency.

You either show up or you don't.

You either get better or stay the same.

There's no middle ground.

You want a better body?

Be consistent.

You want a sharper mind?

Be consistent.

You want financial peace?

Be consistent.

You want self-respect?

Be consistent.

Not for a week.

Not until it gets hard.

Forever.

Because the things that matter most aren't built in one big moment.

They're built in small moments stacked with discipline.

So yeah, show up big.

But more importantly?

Show up again tomorrow.

Chapter 94: It's Supposed to Be Hard

If it was easy, everybody would have it.

Everybody would be locked in.

Everybody would be disciplined.

Everybody would be successful.

But they're not.

Because this path?

It's hard.

And it's supposed to be.

I used to think something was wrong when I struggled.

When I felt tired.

When I didn't want to train, didn't want to write, didn't want to show up.

But I get it now—

That resistance?

That's the price of growth.

Most people back off the second it gets uncomfortable.

They want the body, but not the workouts.

They want the mindset, but not the silence.

They want success, but not the discipline.

They want the rewards, but not the reps.

You lean into it.

Because you know that's where you separate the committed from the curious.

That's where the real growth happens—in the suck, in the grind, in the struggle.

I've lived through enough now to know:

If it's hard, I'm in the right place.

If I'm uncomfortable, I'm building something solid.

If I feel stretched, that means I'm outgrowing the old me.

And that's the goal.

Don't chase easy.

Easy will keep you average.

Chase the hard days.

The ones that test your character.

The ones that expose your excuses.

The ones that feel too heavy—and do it anyway.

You don't need perfect.

You need pressure.

Pressure makes you focused.

Pressure makes you real.

Pressure makes you strong.

So when it gets hard?

Don't panic.

Don't back off.

Just remind yourself:

It's supposed to be this way.

And I'm built for it.

Pressure doesn't just test you.

It trains you.

It teaches you to focus.

To move intentionally.

To remove distraction.

To sharpen your edge.

The moments in my life where I had the most clarity?

Weren't when things were easy.

They were in the middle of chaos.

When everything was on the line.

When I had no backup plan.

No safety net.

Just me, the mission, and the decision to keep going.

That's what pressure does—it strips away the excuses and reveals who you really are.

You start to move different.

You speak less.

You listen more.

You stop chasing attention and start chasing alignment.

You become precise—with your time, with your habits, with your words.

Because pressure doesn't let you waste anything.

You're not looking for comfort.

You're looking for the edge.

And that edge?

Only shows up when things get heavy.

Most people crack under pressure.

They panic.

They stall.

They shut down.

But the ones who are built for more?

They get sharper.

Pressure teaches you to:

Get organized

Cut off distractions

Prioritize growth

Stop playing small

Finish what you start.

The pressure you are under right now?

It is not punishment.

It is preparation.

So do not run from it.

Don't complain about it.

Use it.

Let it refine you.

Let it build precision into how you move.

Pressure builds precision.

And precision builds greatness.

Some days you will wake up with the weight already on you.

Your mind will push back.

Your body will be sore.

Your schedule will not make sense.

And that voice in your head will ask:

"Why is this so hard?"

Here is the answer:

Because it's supposed to be.

Growth is heavy.

Change is uncomfortable.

Discipline is unnatural—for most.

But for you?

It's normal now.

Why keep going?

Because the weight means you are still in it.

Still becoming.

Still rising.

If it were light,

everyone would carry it.

But you are not "everyone."

You are carrying the weight of:

Your name

Your story

Your standard

Your legacy

Of course, it feels heavy.

It is supposed to.

You are carrying discipline in a world that pushes distraction.

You are choosing silence in a world addicted to attention.

You are showing up daily in a culture built on shortcuts.

That kind of weight?

It means you are doing it right.

So, when the days feel thick,

When the reps feel slow,

when the path feels steep—

Smile.

That is your confirmation.

Pressure creates precision.

Weight builds strength.

Hard makes you harder to break.

If it feels heavy, good.

It means you are getting stronger.

It means you are doing it right.

You will lose people when you tighten your habits.

You will be misunderstood when you raise your standard.

You will feel distant when you stop moving like the rest.

That is normal.

That's discipline.

371

This path is supposed to feel lonely.

Most people do not want to do what you're doing.

They want comfort.

They want distraction.

They want excuses that sound smart.

You gave that up.

So yes, it gets quiet.

It gets boring.

It gets isolating.

But that is the price of elevation.

Success, pain, and discipline are not built in crowds.

They are built in silence.

In solitude.

In suffering—when you are the only one showing up.

I have had nights where it felt like nobody understood.

No calls.

No hype.

No check-ins.

Just me, my standard, and the decision to not break it.

You do not need attention.

You need reps.

You need focus.

You need a reason that's bigger than comfort.

Loneliness is part of it.

But so is peace.

So is clarity.

So is strength that does not depend on applause.

Let them go.

Let them doubt.

Let it feel lonely.

You have got something they don't: consistency.

Keep showing up.

Keep pushing.

Keep building.

Even when it is quiet.

Especially when it is quiet.

Discipline feels lonely.

Keep going anyway.

Not every day is going to go your way.

You already know that.

Some days will punch you in the mouth.

You will be tired.

You will feel behind.

You will question if it's worth it.

That's why you train.

You don't train for the easy days.

You train for the ones that try to break you.

You prep your mind for pressure.

You prep your body for resistance.

You build habits that don't break under stress.

That's how you stay dangerous.

Ready for pain.

Ready for setbacks.

Ready for life to swing first—because you will swing back harder.

Me? I have learned to stop wishing for smooth days.

I just prepare for the tough ones.

Because when they come—and they always do—I'm already built for it.

When the schedule changes...

When the workout sucks...

When the silence gets heavy...

I do not flinch.

I fall back on the system I built.

Discipline does not panic.

Discipline does not need ideal conditions.

Discipline just shows up—especially when it's hard.

So don't just build routines for the perfect day.

Build for the storm.

Build for the days where everything feels off.

Because those are the days that test if what you built is real.

And if you're ready for those?

You're ready for anything.

Be ready for the hard days.

They are the ones that define you.

Chapter 95: Progress Over Comfort

Motivation fades.

Emotions shift.

Situations change.

But discipline stays.

That's the difference between people who rise—and people who stop halfway.

Motivation is cool, but it's not reliable.

Some days you feel it.

Most days you don't.

If I waited to feel motivated, I wouldn't be where I am now.

I'd still be stuck hoping instead of working.

Discipline is what got me here.

It's what got me through boot camp.

Through college.

Through late nights and early mornings.

Through stress, silence, and setbacks.

Discipline isn't about being perfect.

It's about being committed.

It's waking up tired—and showing up anyway.

It's studying when the room is chaotic, when your mind is cloudy, when you're not in the mood.

It's saying no to what's easy so you can say yes to what's earned.

Every time I followed through when I didn't feel like it—I grew.

Not just physically.

Mentally.

I became more durable.

Calmer.

Sharper.

More focused.

People want to know the shortcut.

There isn't one.

The answer is discipline.

Every time.

I don't need distraction.

I need routine.

I don't need energy.

I need structure.

I don't need praise.

I need purpose.

Discipline isn't a phase—it's a lifestyle.

It's who you become when nobody's watching.

It's the voice in your head that says,

"We don't skip. We don't back down. We don't give up."

And here's the truth:

No matter where life takes me...

No matter what changes...

Discipline comes with me.

It's in my bones now.

It's non-negotiable.

It's how I live.

How I move.

How I lead.

Discipline is forever.

And I'm never letting it go.

It's easy to make promises when you're motivated.

"I'm going to wake up early."

"I'm going to stop messing around."

"I'm going to change my life."

But when the feeling fades?

Do you follow through?

The hardest person to stay loyal to... is you.

Because no one's holding you accountable but you.

No one's checking to see if you got it done.

No one's calling you out when you slack—except your reflection.

I used to break promises to myself all the time.

Start strong, fall off.

Say I'd quit something, then justify it.

Say I'd wake up early, then snooze ten times.

And every time I did that?

I trained my mind that my word didn't mean much.

But when I started honoring my word—even in private?

Everything changed.

I built trust with myself.

And that trust?

That's where self-respect comes from.

Not the gym.

Not the outfit.

Not the post.

But from doing what you said—when nobody's around to applaud it.

That's exactly what keeping your word to yourself is.

It's a war.

Between your potential and your patterns.

Your discipline and your excuses.

Your goals and your comfort.

Every time you do what you said—even when you don't feel like it—you win that war.

You stack confidence.

You build internal strength.

You move like someone who can't be broken—because you don't lie to yourself.

If you say you're going to wake up—get up.

If you say you're going to train—train.

If you say you're going to cut people off—cut them off.

If you say you're locked in—prove it.

To yourself first.

Forget the crowd.

Forget the followers.

You know who sees you when the lights are off?

You.

So, if you want to feel strong again?

Start keeping the promises you make in silence.

Start respecting the commitments no one else hears.

That's where real power is built.

Keep your word to yourself.

Every day.

No excuses.

You don't have to announce everything.

You don't have to explain your every move.

You don't have to convince people to believe in you.

You don't need their validation.

You just need to show up—and let the work speak.

Because here's the truth:

Results silence everything.

The doubters get quiet.

The ones who ghosted start watching.

The ones who clowned you start mimicking you.

And you don't even have to say a word.

That is how you become undeniable.

Not through noise.

Not through arguments.

Not through drama.

Just consistency.

Just action.

Just execution—daily.

I used to want people to "get it."

Now I do not care who gets it.

I just stay focused.

And people see the difference.

They see the discipline.

They feel the shift.

Because when the work is real,

you don't have to say a thing.

So keep stacking.

Keep showing up.

Keep your circle tight.

Keep your head down.

Because the ones who matter will notice.

And the ones who doubted?

They will get quiet eventually.

Let the results talk.

And let your silence hit louder than their opinions.

The ones you feel like doing?

The ones you don't.

The hard ones.

The quiet ones.

They all matter.

It's easy to think one missed day won't matter.

One skipped rep.

One shortcut.

But that's how average gets built—one excuse at a time.

On the flip side?

Excellence is built the same way.

One early wake-up.

One more page.

One more set.

One more time saying "no" when it's easier to say "yes."

And every step added weight to the foundation.

I've learned to stop counting big wins.

I count the small ones:

I showed up.

I pushed through.

I didn't skip the extra round.

I got it done when no one would've blamed me for taking a break.

That's where I win.

You don't need to be perfect.

But you do need to be honest.

Honest with your effort.

Honest with your excuses.

Honest with your standard.

So if the workout wasn't perfect—did you finish?

If the study session was short—did you lock in?

If your day got hectic—did you still honor the minimum?

Because every rep counts.

Not just physically.

Mentally.

Emotionally.

Spiritually.

Small wins stack into momentum.

Momentum turns into identity.

Identity turns into legacy.

Every rep counts.

Stop skipping.

Start stacking.

You can want it bad.

You can write it on your mirror.

Put it on your wall.

Set it as your phone wallpaper.

But wanting something doesn't get it done.

Repeating the right actions does.

Motivation comes and goes.

Goals can shift.

But your habits?

That's your real identity.

If you eat clean once a week—

You're not disciplined.

If you train hard once a month—

You're not locked in.

If you study when it's convenient—
You're not serious.

You don't rise to your level of vision.
You fall to the level of your daily reps.

You want a stronger body?
Repeat training.
You want a sharper mind?
Repeat reading, writing, reflecting.
You want discipline?
Repeat the hard choice.
Every day.
Not just when you're feeling it.

What you do once doesn't matter.
What you do always does.

So check yourself:
What are you repeating?
What patterns are shaping your outcomes?
Are your habits matching your goals?

Because talk is cheap.
Repetition is real.

Don't just want it.

Don't just say it.

Repeat it—until it becomes who you are.

You don't get what you want.

You get what you repeat.

Chapter 96: Remember Who You Are

When it gets hard again—and it will...

When people doubt you again—and they will...

When your body says stop, and your mind says quit...

Remember.

You've done the work.

You've earned this mind.

You've survived worse.

You've stayed locked when it was quiet.

That means something.

This isn't motivation.

This is your identity now.

Discipline isn't a trend—it's your default.

Pressure isn't new—it's your fuel.

Silence isn't lonely—it's where you sharpen.

You built that.

And it's yours to carry—into every room, every situation,
every storm.

People will forget what you did.
 They'll overlook the reps.
 They'll ignore the early mornings.
 They'll downplay the comeback.

Let them.

But you?

You don't forget.

You don't break.
 You don't flinch.
 You don't back down.

This mindset?
 This focus?

This pain-tested, pressure-built, earned-through-every-hard-day discipline?

This is you now.

You don't have to prove it.
Just keep living it.

And every time life tests you again—

Remember who you are.

Chapter 97: The Work Is Never Over

This book might be ending—
But the grind isn't.

The discipline you've built?
It doesn't stop here.

It just moves with you into the next thing.

Because real work never finishes.

There's always another level.
Another test.
Another day to stay locked in when everything says ease up.

Because that's where you stay sharp.

That's where you stay dangerous.

You didn't come this far to chill.
You came this far to confirm who you are.

And that identity?

Needs to be reinforced daily.

Not because you're not enough.
But because you're not done.

Not even close.

So whatever comes next—

School.
Work.
Family.
Business.
Health.
Leadership.

Bring this version of you to it.
The focused one.
The grounded one.
The built-not-born one.

This wasn't just a season.
It's a standard.

And now that you've raised it?

You never drop it again.

The book might close.

But the work?

It keeps going.

The work is never over.
And neither are you.

Epilogue: Keep Going

You held these pages.
You walked through every chapter.
You saw the mindset, the pain, the fire.
Not just mine—
But yours, too.

Because if you saw yourself in any of this,
it means you're ready to take your own discipline further.

This wasn't a motivational story.
It was a reminder:
You don't need perfect conditions.
You don't need permission.
You don't need anyone to save you.

You just need pressure.
And follow-through.

If you made it this far?

You already know what to do next.

Close this book.
And keep going.

Acknowledgment

I want to thank David Goggins—not just for his story, but for how he lives it. His example helped me stay focused when things got heavy. His mindset pushed me when I could have settled. I have never met him, but his work showed me what it means to go beyond what you think you are capable of. This book exists, in part, because of that influence.

David Goggins is mentioned in this memoir as a source of inspiration. Those references come from deep respect for his work and the impact it has had on my life.

www.ingramcontent.com/pod-product-compliance
Lightning Source LLC
Chambersburg PA
CBHW051257120626
46547CB00015B/1975